Pineapple Passion

B-107

by Nancy Smith & Lynda Milligan

DEDICATION

We would like to dedicate this book to our parents who inspired us to become the women that we are today and to strive for what we want from our tomorrows, to the memories of our fathers who supported us in years past, and to our mothers who continue to love and support us as we venture forth to fulfill our dreams. We love you!

Rich and Aina Martin
Don Staudacher and Ava Staudacher Risser

ACKNOWLEDGMENTS

Special thanks to:

Quiltmakers Ruth Haggbloom, Opal Homersham, Sharon Holmes, Nancy J. Martin, Janet Robinson, and Kathy Simes for their patterns.

Quiltmakers Charlotte Ballard, Mary Jo Dalrymple, Linda Nolte Evans, Janice Hagan, Joanne Malone, Shirley Sanden, Christine Scott, Sharon West, and Terri Wiley for their photographs.

Quilt collectors Luella Doss, Bryce and Donna Hamilton, Sandy Pape, and Sandra Wolf.

Quilters Gwen Michal, Connie Powell, Saloma Yoder, and Daphne Wells.

Our supportive, generous, and encouraging friends Peggie Hudiburg, Helen Hall, Dick Rogers, Jean Yancey, and Linda Calkins.

Our invaluable contributors Jane Dumler, Judy Carpenter, Bev Thuer, Marilyn Robinson, Peggie Van Zandt, Mary Bourn, Alison Minor, Osie Lebowitz, Peg Spike, Karen Wilborn, and Aina Martin.

CREDITS

Photography . . . . Brent Kane
Illustration and Graphics . . . . Stephanie Benson
Text and Cover Design . . . . Judy Petry
Editor . . . . Liz McGehee

Pineapple Passion©
That Patchwork Place, Inc., Bothell, WA 98041
© 1989 by Nancy Smith and Lynda Milligan

Printed in the British Crown Colony of Hong Kong
96 95 94 93 92 91 90 89   6 5 4 3 2 1

Library of Congress Cataloging-in-Publication Data

Smith, Nancy, 1943 Oct. 17-
    Pineapple passion / Nancy Smith, Lynda Milligan.
        p.   cm.
        ISBN 0-943574-60-9
        1. Quilting—Patterns. 2. Patchwork—Patterns. I. Milligan, Lynda, 1951- . II. Title.
TT835.S57 1989
746.9'7—dc20   88-51684
                                                    CIP

Contents

Introduction

Log Cabin is a traditional quilt design with ever-lasting appeal. This pattern is a favorite because of its versatility: It can be made with any fabric and is a good way to utilize scraps; its well-planned design can be very colorful; and it is easy to put together.

Pineapple, a variation of Log Cabin, has never held the same popularity. Very little has been written about the Pineapple pattern, and relatively few antique quilts have been found. However, a simple method of constructing Pineapple quilts has created a new appeal for this wonderful pattern.

You are about to embark on an exciting and wonderful new approach to Pineapple quiltmaking. Our template-free method for making Pineapple quilts eliminates all the tediousness of making tiny, multitudinous templates to piece one Pineapple block. As the title of this book implies, you are likely to develop a passion, an indescribable taste, for Pineapple patterns in all sizes, shapes, variations, and flavors.

The refinement of our technique came about through the invaluable feedback we received from members of the Colorado Quilt Council, Arapahoe County Quilters, and our own Great American Quilt Factory customers and employees.

Excitement, ease, simplicity, joy, and fun is yours for the taking. Sit down, read through the book and imagine yourself on a journey. Your first stop on your "road to success" in Pineapple quiltmaking will be discovering the *Tools and Supplies* that will make this quilt easy and fun. One of these tools, the Pineapple Rule, has been specifically designed to help guarantee perfect Pineapple blocks. Its unique feature is the series of 45° angles radiating from the center line.

Your next stop will be choosing *Fabrics*. Begin to think about the special effect that you can create with out-of-the-ordinary fabrics that will make your quilt unusual and unique. Along the way you will find several *Design and Color* exercises that will challenge you to explore your own Pineapple creativity. You will experiment with penciled drawings and fabric paste-ups. Be sure to devote extra attention to *Assembling a Pineapple Block*. All Pineapple patterns in the book are based on this distinctive technique.

The *Gallery of Quilts* beginning on page 25 is included to inspire, delight, and energize you. It is a celebration of creative talent from women in past and present generations. From here you choose the direction to travel. Select one of the quilt patterns that will express your "Pineapple Passion" or venture into uncharted territory and design your own. For those readers unfamiliar with quiltmaking, refer to the *Glossary of Techniques* for instruction on specific techniques, such as machine piecing, quilting, and the final step of binding.

Making Pineapple quilts with this new method is wonderful and addictive in the most positive sense of the word. An exciting and different world of quiltmaking is about to unfold for you.

Tools and Supplies

PINEAPPLE RULE/SEE-THROUGH RULERS

Most people seem to develop a preference for one kind of ruler or another. One person will prefer a ruler with raised ridges on the underneath side, while another person will prefer a smooth surface because the lines are finer. There is really no better or best ruler, but do choose one that fits your specific needs and one with which you feel comfortable. Certain rulers have been devised for specific needs or purposes, such as the Bias Square™, which is used to construct half-square triangles, or a Pineapple Rule, which greatly eases the cutting and construction of Pineapple blocks.

With the Pineapple Rule, you can make perfect Pineapple blocks. This ruler has many features that will make construction easier. Radiating from a center line, 45° angles are marked in ¼" increments. These markings are essential for accurate cutting guides. Horizontal and vertical lines, marked at least every inch, serve as guidelines for sewing, as well as for measuring and cutting strips and squares. These guidelines help ensure accuracy for this template-free technique. The 12" length is easy to handle, and the thickness stabilizes the cutter. If you choose not to use this special rule, there are adaptations you can make to other rulers. Using a 45° angle and a scribe (available in hardware stores), you can mark extra lines on your ruler (see ruler diagram). The most important lines are the center vertical and the inside row of 45° angles, as well as a few more 45° angles. Essentially, you are "etching in" extra lines. Even though these lines are clear, you can still see them on your fabric. However, if you would like to darken them, color them with a permanent marking pen, wiping off any extra ink with a paper towel. Pineapple Rules are available from DreamSpinners, 8970 E. Hampden Ave., Denver, CO 80231.

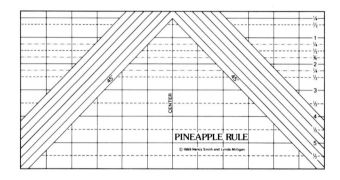

ROTARY CUTTER

This rolling disk blade cuts easily through fabric without hand fatigue. These cutters come with large or small blades; both work equally well. However, the small replacement blades are usually less expensive than the large ones.

CUTTING MAT

You will want a mat made especially for use with the rotary cutter; it has a self-healing surface. The mats vary in size from 4" square to approximately 23" x 35". The most usable size for making Pineapple quilts is a mat that measures at least 23" wide, enabling you to cut a width of folded 45" fabric.

SCISSORS

Sharp scissors are a must for any kind of sewing. If you choose to use scissors rather than a rotary cutter to cut your strips, be sure to cut only as many layers as will cut smoothly and accurately. Anytime your scissors begin to bind, your fabric will shift, and you will not get perfect strips.

SEWING MACHINE

You can use any straight-stitch sewing machine to sew Pineapple quilts. A ¼″ seam guide is absolutely essential. If the edge of your pressure foot is exactly ¼″ from the needle, you can use it as a guide; otherwise the throat plate must be marked or the needle position moved. An even-feed foot is also helpful for sewing through several thicknesses. When applying binding or stitching through batting, fleece, needlepunch, etc., an even-feed foot prevents slippage. Most sewing machine dealers carry them for their particular brand machine.

THREAD

For sewing machine work, a strong polyester or cotton-covered polyester thread works best. It is usually easiest to sew with a neutral color throughout: light with lights, dark with darks. For quilting thread, you may choose between cotton, cotton-covered, and polyester. All seem to work fine, and what you use is only a matter of preference.

NEEDLES

Hand sewing needles are sold as "sharps." The higher the number, the finer the needle. Quilting needles are called "betweens." They also are sold according to number, and again, the higher the number, the finer the needle. Both sharps and betweens range from #5–#12. We personally find finer needles easier to sew with, but they are also harder to thread.

IRON AND IRONING BOARD

A good steam iron is essential for pressing the bars of the Pineapple block. An ironing board cover with a marked grid is also helpful. Make sure the cover is straight and use it as a pressing guide.

REDUCING GLASS

This looks like a magnifying glass but is actually the exact opposite. It makes your work look smaller rather than larger and will help you focus on your project without background interference. Often, problem areas become evident when you view your work from a distance. Reducing glasses are usually available through art or drafting supply stores or perhaps your local quilt store. You can achieve the same effect by looking through the opposite end of a pair of binoculars or through a camera lens.

COLORED PENCILS

Any brand of pencils will work, but a set with a wide range of colors is the most helpful. You can get different shades by pressing lighter or harder on the pencil point. Also, coloring over an already-colored area can increase your color possibilities.

WONDER-UNDER™ TRANSFER WEBBING

This transfuse webbing, manufactured by Pellon, makes paper, fabric, wood, cardboard, etc., fusible. It is available through fabric and craft stores and is generally sold by the yard.

MIRRORS

By using two 12″ mirror tiles set at right angles, you will be able to see what one block reflected into four images looks like. You can use this technique for viewing colored pencil drawings and fabric paste-ups, as well as sewn blocks.

Fabric

The recommended fabric content for quilting is 100% cotton. There are a number of reasons for using all-cotton fabrics. First, they are natural fibers. As the quilt ages, the various fabrics tend to wear at similar rates. Cotton fibers have similar "stretchability," and they iron well. They are easy to quilt through. The patina and softness of aging cotton is unbeatable!

The fabric should be of similar lightweight or dress-weight, closely woven cotton. You may find that you need to use a fabric other than 100% cotton for design or color variation. Notice that the Reflections quilt on page 59 incorporates gold lamé center squares for a stunning visual accent. The texture of fabrics, such as corduroy or velveteen, can create unusual and subtle colorings, depending on how the nap reflects the light. Just be aware of the unique characteristics of the fabrics you use, such as colorfastness, washability, etc.

Pineapple quilts can use any printed or plain fabric. The combinations are innumerable. Large prints work as well as small-scale calicoes. Special effects can be created by using specific design elements found in many of the contemporary prints. Selective cutting and positioning to incorporate particular design components lead to artistic results (i.e., animal heads, flowers, lettering, eyes, leaves, characters, etc.). Some things to consider when choosing fabrics are scale and similarity of prints; directional prints, such as stripes and plaids; and repeat motifs. Stripes, although a little more time-consuming, can produce dramatic results. They can be cut vertically, horizontally, and diagonally. We have effectively used stripes in the logs as well as in borders.

Determine if washable fabrics are colorfast by hand-washing separately in detergent and warm water. If the water remains clear, fabrics may be washed together. If any fabric bleeds, wash it separately. If fabric continues to bleed, discard and select another fabric. After checking for colorfastness, wash fabrics in a washing machine with warm water and a mild detergent; rinse well. Tumble dry, as most shrinkage usually occurs in the dryer. Press, using steam and spray-sizing, if necessary.

Design and Color

The resemblance of the Pineapple block to the fruit is apparent in the angularity of the design. One can almost see the jagged edges of the leaves and the plumpness of the fruit. There is generally one basic line design for the Pineapple pattern. However, as in Log Cabin, there are many possible variations. When you construct the block, the dynamic impact will depend on the number, color, and width of logs.

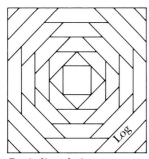

Basic line design

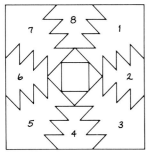

Eight arms and center square

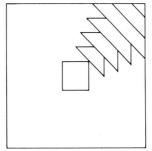

One arm showing individual logs

The Pineapple block itself is made up of eight arms and a center square. The center square can be left as a square or broken up into smaller squares, triangles, etc. Each arm contains a specific number of logs. These logs can vary by number and width. Increasing the number of logs allows for more color variation and creative expression and will create a larger block.

Pineapples having a very large number of logs are sometimes called "Windmill" or "Windmill Blades." Generally, the log width remains constant but can be very effective when changed. (See center of Victoriana quilt, page 51, and the Mosaic wall quilt, page 45.)

Most of the antique Pineapple quilts were made with very narrow bars, ½"–¾" wide, probably from the necessity to use even the smallest of scraps. Because of the availability of fabric today, we have the option of using larger pieces. Wide logs can be very appealing and can make the quilt much quicker and easier to sew.

Color is a very important variable in Pineapple patterns. Because they have eight arms and a variable number of logs per arm, the option for color exploration is incredible. The beauty of the Pineapple is that you can choose to make it as simple or as complex as you like. As can be seen from photographs in this book, the graphic strength of two-color Pineapple quilts is elegant, traditional, and bold. They are clean and fresh, making a superb statement of simplicity. If you choose to use more colors, your possibilities become endless. Visualize the diagonal arms one color, the vertical and horizontal arms a second color, and the center square and corners a third color. Within each arm, you can use shades of a color.

Scraps make a delightful statement. Working with color and the Pineapple pattern is like opening a brand new box of 120 Crayola® crayons—exciting, beautiful, begging to be used—but where do you begin?

We have designed a few exercises to help you find some color combination take-off points. Often, beginning is the hardest step, and hopefully, these exercises, beginning on the next page, will gently nudge you into some color creativity and exploration. You will need a set of colored pencils with a variety of colors. Make several copies of the Four-Block Coloring Diagrams on page 76. Begin to explore the possibilities! Use the work sheets on pages 78 and 79 to expand your design to a full-size quilt.

TWO-COLOR BLOCKS

1. Color all center squares and diagonal arms one color and all vertical and horizontal arms another color (Illustration 1). Notice the proportion of colors: There is more navy than brown.

Illustration 1

2. Color the same as in Illustration 1, but this time, change the last two logs of the diagonal arms to the opposite color. Notice how it breaks up the dominant color and seems to give more of an equal color balance (Illustration 2).

Illustration 2

3. Color diagonals blue, except for rows 9 and 10. Leave center square, verticals, and horizontals white. (See Blue Willow quilt, page 57.) The graphic impact of the spikes becomes the dramatic focus. With the corners and center squares the same color, the pattern loses the traditionally predominant circles (Illustration 3).

Illustration 3

4. Color verticals, horizontals, and diagonal log rows 8 and 10 one color, and color the center and remaining diagonals another color. You will see a square resembling a bull's-eye where the four blocks meet in the center. This bull's-eye may be used as a design element in your quilt (Illustration 4).

Illustration 4

5. Color the center and diagonals through log 8 of blocks A and D one color. Also color horizontals, verticals, and diagonals 9 and 10 of blocks B and C. Leave the remaining logs white. These simple changes give a whole new appearance to the block: The Pineapple block is lost, and your eye keeps moving, trying to find the pattern (Illustration 5).

Illustration 5

As you can see, two colors can be combined in numerous ways. None is right or wrong—only different. You can choose what feels best for you. Trust your feelings. They are good indicators of what colors are right for you.

THREE-COLOR BLOCKS

1. Try one horizontal/vertical color and two different diagonal colors. The center square can be either of the diagonal colors (Illustration 6).

Illustration 6

2. Repeat coloring as in step 1, cut blocks apart, and turn blocks B and C 90°. You will notice one color concentrated in the center (Illustration 7).

Illustration 7

Now is a fun time to experiment with the mirror tiles. This trick will save you hours of design and sewing time and is well worth the investment. Be sure to tape the edges to avoid cutting yourself. Set the mirrors upright at right angles to each other. Prop them up with books and tape the corners or make a stand. The mirrors should fit flush together and to the surface. Set your colored drawing in the corner where the mirrors meet. Stand back and you will see a four–reflection image of your design. Squint your eyes slightly to see hidden patterns emerge. Notice how the ring pattern surrounds the medallions of color. Go back through your colored drawings now and see how the patterns interact. **Note:** You will see only mirror images of your drawings. Thus, illustrations 5 and 6 will not reflect accurate layouts.

3. Color center square and diagonal corners one color. Color remaining diagonals a second color and horizontals and verticals a third color. The focus changes from a single focal point to a double one—the centers of blocks and corners. For an interesting variation, see Kathy Simes' Mosaic quilt, page 45. Kathy has reduced the width of log 8 and created a less powerful bull's-eye effect (Illustration 8).

Illustration 8

4. You do not need to use the same fabric to create this three-color effect. You can use various shades of a color, as shown in the Pine Needles quilt on page 39. The black/green prints are in the same color family and act as one color.

FOUR OR MORE COLORS

1. Color the left-hand diagonal one color, the right-hand diagonal a second color, the horizontal a third, and the vertical a fourth. Color the center square the same color as either of the diagonals. Place your drawing in the mirror. Ignore your diagonal colors, but note how the horizontals and verticals form bands (Illustration 9). (See Tapestry quilt, page 55.)

Illustration 9

2. Color blocks in your choice of colors. Note the line bands of color that form. Place in mirrors to see what a repeat design would look like (Illustration 10).

Illustration 10

3. Hopefully, the multi-colored designs in illustrations 11–14 will inspire your color creativity. Illustration 11 suggests rainbow sherbet.

Illustration 11

Illustration 13

Illustration 12

Illustration 14

4. Experiment with four or more colors. This experimentation is addictive, and you can get hooked on just coloring. However, it is time to move on.

Illustration 15

Fabric Block 1   *Fabric Block 2*

FABRIC PASTE-UPS

1. Color a set of four blocks as shown in Illustration 15. From this coloring, choose two fabrics and make a "paste-up." To make a paste-up, cut 1″ strips of your fabrics. Make two copies of the paste-up guide (page 74). Tape halves together, matching dotted lines.

   Cut a piece of Pellon Wonder-Under™ the size of the line drawing. Following manufacturer's instructions, fuse it to your paper. Peel off paper covering Wonder-Under™. Trim 1″ fabric strips to fit desired logs. Lay fabric strips on drawing. Press to fuse in place.

   Coloring is easy, quick, and changeable. Fabric strips are inexpensive, quick to paste up, and easy to change and alter. Use your mirrors again for viewing potential quilt layouts. Our blue- and white-colored drawing translated into fabric is shown in fabric blocks 1 and 2.

2. Color a block as shown (Illustration 16).

Illustration 16

Translate this block into your fabric choices. We chose the combination shown in Fabric Block 3. Set this block in your mirrors. We found that the purple coming together with the watercolor fabric surrounding it was marvelous. However, the pink looked too orange; it needed a rosier pink. We simply cut a different pink and laid it over the top (Fabric Block 4). See if you don't agree that this pink is more pleasing.

Fabric Block 3   *Fabric Block 4*

Another possible combination is shown in Illustration 17.

Our translation into fabrics is shown in fabric blocks 5 and 6. We like Fabric Block 5 better; Fabric Block 6 does not show enough contrast. We were not sure of the light center in either block but decided to experiment with it. See what you can come up with to enhance the color combinations of this design.

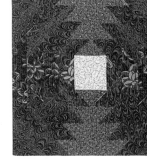

Fabric Block 5   *Fabric Block 6*   *Illustration 17*

3. It can be fun to work with stripes. Shown in Illustration 18 are two different three-color blocks. Opposite colors alternate diagonally from the center. Horizontals and verticals are the third color. Our fabric interpretation uses a stripe. Both interpretations work well when reflected in the mirrors (fabric blocks 7 and 8). Notice the mitering of the stripes in these blocks.

Illustration 18

Fabric Block 7   *Fabric Block 8*

Illustration 19 shows three different ways that these two blocks can be assembled.

Illustration 19

4. Illustration 20 shows the progression of changes in arriving at our final color selections. We chose fabrics loosely interpreting the colors in the drawing.

Illustration 20

Using the mirrors, we viewed Fabric Block 9 in a four-block arrangement. The green and peach were fine, but the purple seemed too heavy and did not appeal to us. We replaced the purple with a green check by cutting strips and simply laying them over the purple. The result is shown in Fabric Block 10, which we think is a pleasing combination. However, while we liked the peach centers coming together, we were less satisfied with the heavy concentration of green check. So, in Fabric Block 11, we darkened the peach fabric; it toned down the green check and gave the block more color balance. Our final combination was light and dark peach (Fabric Block 12).

Fabric Block 9   *Fabric Block 10*

Fabric Block 11   *Fabric Block 12*

Fabric Block 13

Fabric Block 14

Fabric Block 15

Fabric Block 16

FABRIC BLOCK SET-UPS

Using actual fabric blocks, we have made several different arrangements to show how colors can be emphasized or de-emphasized. By squinting or looking through a reducing glass, you can see the predominant patterns emerge. Using the same three fabrics, four different blocks are shown in fabric blocks 13, 14, 15, and 16.

We have used these four blocks to make six different combinations on pages 16–19. You undoubtedly will come up with several more. Examine each set and decide what pleases or displeases you about each. We hope that this exercise will help you design your own unique Pineapple quilt.

First Combination. All blocks are the same.

Second Combination.
All blocks are the same.

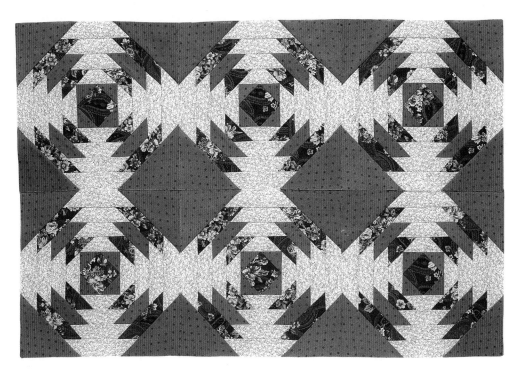

Third Combination.
Colors alternate to tan corners.

Fourth Combination.
Floral corners alternate.

Fifth Combination. Tan corners alternate with floral corners.

Sixth Combination. Tan rows alternate with floral rows.

As you can see, the combinations are numerous. Remember, there is no right or wrong way but only what you prefer. The overall tone is the same for all of these combinations, but the colors are distributed differently. If you like the floral print, you will probably want to emphasize it, or vice versa for the tan. These easy techniques of experimenting with color allow you room to play.

Cutting Techniques

Accuracy is so important and essential to having a successful Pineapple-making adventure. There is nothing difficult about this technique, but it is dependent on accuracy. You will be building out from the center, and if one strip is cut incorrectly, the mistake will be compounded with every log. The tell-tale time will come when you attempt to set the blocks together. If you can sew accurate ¼″ seams and cut very straight strips and squares, you can make perfect Pineapple quilts!

1. Squares and strips may be cut with scissors or, more quickly, with ruler, rotary cutter, and cutting mat.
2. Layer cut only as many layers as will cut easily and accurately without slipping. Don't rush—take your time.
3. For scissor cutting, mark width of strips with sharp pencil or chalk marker and cut on the lines.
4. For rotary cutting, begin by laying wrinkle-free folded fabric on your cutting mat. Position it so the fold and selvage are parallel to your body, one on top of the other, layering four thicknesses.

    Be sure fold and selvages are even. Using your Pineapple Rule or a "see-through" ruler marked with a right angle, match up the top of the ruler or one of the right-angle lines with the fold of the fabric.

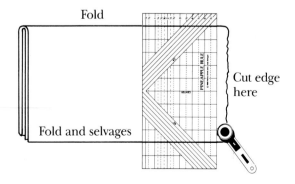

Cut the right edge of the fabric off, which will give you a straight edge from which to begin.

5. Swing your fabric or, even better, your mat around 180°. You are now ready to cut your strips.
6. Position ruler so that the marking for your strip width is even with the edges of the fabric. Keep the top and bottom edges of fabric even with horizontal lines of the ruler. Run the cutter along the right edge of the ruler.

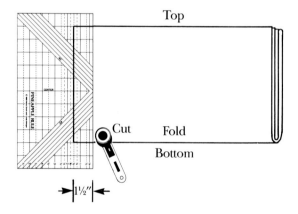

Open out this strip to check for straightness. If the strip is wavy, refold your fabric and realign the fold with the selvage.

7. Cut the strips into log sizes for your particular quilt. We have allowed extra length for some slight stitching discrepancies. Cutting strips into logs and setting them next to your machine in numerical piecing order will make it easy to put your blocks together quickly and accurately.

Assembling a Pineapple Block
Using the Template-Free Method

Again, accuracy is of utmost importance. Your Pineapple blocks will be only as accurate as the time you put into preparation and sewing. Seam allowances are ¼″. We have included a ¼″ seam guide here to help you adjust the seam width of your machine. Trace or copy the guide onto paper. Cut it out and insert it under your presser foot as if you were going to sew. Without thread in the needle, hand wheel the needle into the paper at the seam line. If you are going to use your presser foot as a guide, it must line up with the edge of the paper guide. If it does not, you may be able to adjust your needle position. If you cannot adjust it, use the paper guide to position a piece of masking tape or, if presser foot is too narrow, use a thin strip of foam moleskin on the throat plate. (Moleskin is available in grocery stores or drugstores.) The thickness of the moleskin keeps your fabric from slipping past the ¼″. As you sew, check your seams now and then with this seam guide.

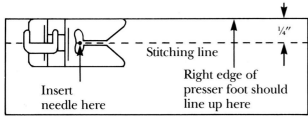

Seam guide

Use ¼″ seam allowances throughout. If you have never tried this method before, it is best to experiment with a practice block before beginning on a whole quilt. Follow the step-by-step directions carefully, and your results will be successful. Remember, accuracy is extremely important. Limit color choices to white and one color (red is used in the example), until you feel comfortable making these blocks.

1. Cut three white strips 2″ wide (1½″ finished) and cut three red strips 2″ wide (1½″ finished) and one red strip 3″ wide. Refer to cutting techniques on page 20.

2. For one block, cut:

White

Center square	1 square	3½″ x 3½″
Row 2	4 logs	2″ x 5½″
Row 4	4 logs	2″ x 6½″
Row 6	4 logs	2″ x 8″

Red

Row 1	4 logs	2″ x 3½″
Row 3	4 logs	2″ x 5½″
Row 5	4 logs	2″ x 6½″
Row 7	4 logs	2″ x 8″
Row 8	4 logs	3″ x 5″

3. Cut center square, either by using the cutting guide provided on page 75 or the Pineapple Rule and rotary cutter. To make sure the center is square, draw a diagonal line from one corner to the opposite corner on the wrong side of the fabric. Use a sharp pencil. Line up the penciled line with a vertical line marked on your Pineapple Rule or other ruler and draw a line to make your angle 90°. If your square is square, your penciled lines will extend from corner to corner both ways. If they do not, recut and mark another square.

4. Lay out strips to the right of your sewing machine in numerical order. Using a neutral-color thread and following the piecing diagram, sew 2″ x 3½″ red logs to all four sides of the center square. Sew top and bottom logs first and then sides. Remember to sew with accurate ¼″ seam allowances. Press seams out carefully, being careful not to stretch the square out of shape. Use guides on ironing board pad, if available, to keep your square and logs as straight as

possible. Make sure the intersecting lines in the center still form a right angle.

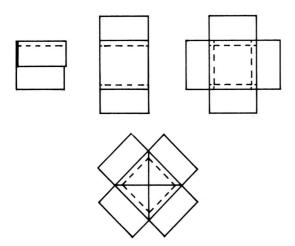

5. Lay your Pineapple Rule or see-through ruler on your block. Line up as many vertical, horizontal, and diagonal markings as possible. The center vertical line needs to match your marked center line. Horizontal lines may not fall exactly on seam lines but need to be parallel and equidistant from seam lines. Diagonal (45°) lines should fall on your stitching lines. You will need to set one standard (S.O.S.). In order to have all your blocks square and the same size, match the lines on all sides of this block and, if making a quilt, on all subsequent blocks. As can be seen from the numbers on the illustration, the Pineapple Rule picks up four distinct guide lines. Center vertical line #1; left and right 45° angles, #2 and #3; and horizontal guide #4. Using your rotary cutter, trim off the corners as shown. Swing your block 90° and repeat this process. Remember, line up the same four guides and trim the corners as before. Swing block again and repeat. Then turn it one last time, and your block should look like the one below. You now have a white center with four red logs in Row 1.

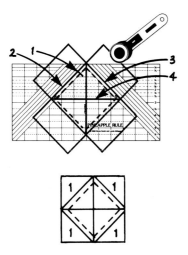

6. Using the ¼″ seam allowance, sew on the four 2″ x 5½″ white logs, sewing from edge to edge. Draw two more lines through centers, corner to corner, again keeping a right angle in the center where the lines cross.

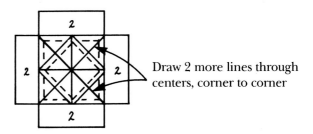

Draw 2 more lines through centers, corner to corner

7. Trim four corners. Again, S.O.S. for cutting by matching the diagonals (45° angles) and the vertical center line. Find a horizontal cross line that you can use as a guide to follow for each side of the block. If you are making a full quilt, match diagonal and vertical center lines as in step 5 and set the same horizontal guide for each side of every block. After adding next row, set a new standard (S.O.S.).

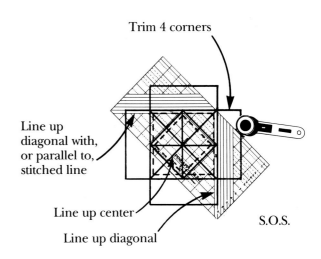

Trim 4 corners

Line up diagonal with, or parallel to, stitched line

Line up center

Line up diagonal

S.O.S.

The wrong side of your block will now look like this:

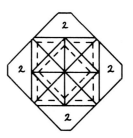

You have just added the second row of logs.

8. Add four 2″ x 5½″ logs of red, sewing with accurate ¼″ seam allowances. Press, being careful not to stretch the block. Trim the four corners. For first cut, line up edge and center. Parallel the diagonals and set a new horizontal guide. Remember, S.O.S.

Add 4 logs

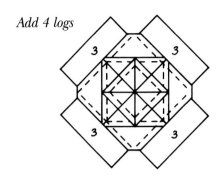

Trim 4 corners

For first cut, line up edge

Parallel diagonals

Set horizontal guide

S.O.S.

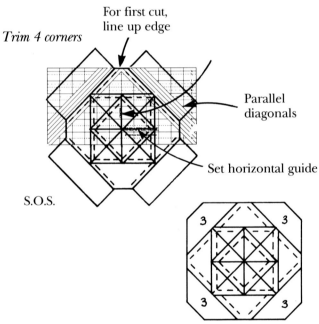

9. Add four 2″ x 6½″ logs of white. Trim corners. For first cut, line up edge, center, and parallels. Continuing with the same guides and following S.O.S. rule, rotate block and cut.

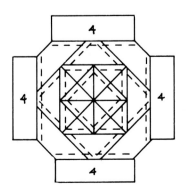

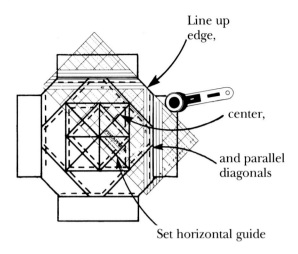

Line up edge,

center,

and parallel diagonals

Set horizontal guide

Note: To follow all guides, you may need to trim a bit or extend an edge; i.e., you may have to move your ruler up or down away from the edge of the fabric in order to match your guidelines, as shown in lower drawing. This inaccuracy may be due to incorrect seam allowance, pressing, stretching, etc. Trimming or extending an edge is a way to compensate, so all blocks remain square and equal.

Cut here

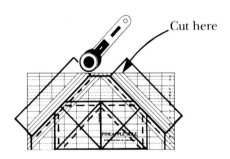

This is what the wrong side of your block will look like after you complete Row 4 of logs.

Trim 4 corners

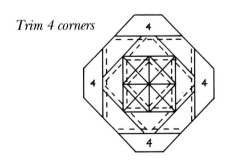

10. Add four 2″ x 6½″ red logs (Row 5). Trim four corners. Line up edge, center, and parallels. Remember, you may have to extend or trim in order to keep your S.O.S.

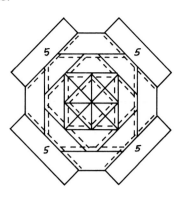

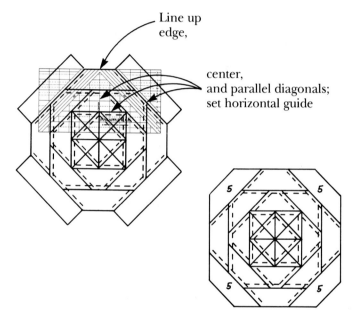

Line up edge,

center, and parallel diagonals; set horizontal guide

11. Continue in this manner, adding red and white logs alternately through Row 7. Your block should look like this:

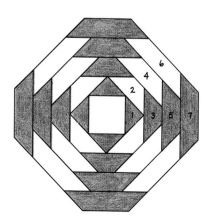

You are now at a decision point in the construction of your block. You can choose to have the red go out to the sides or diagonally to the corners. Lay your block in your mirrors as shown. The red will appear in a horizontal/vertical position. Fill in the empty corner with a white scrap. How do you like it? Turn the block 45° to concentrate the red in the center of the mirror as shown. Fill in the corner with a red scrap. Which do you prefer? We decided to continue with the latter, which makes the center square on point. Refer to pages 78 and 79 to see how full-size quilts would look with center squares straight and on point.

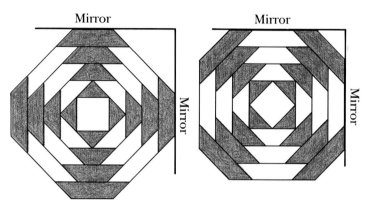

Mirror   Mirror

Mirror   Mirror

12. Sew 3″ x 5″ red logs for four corners; press.
13. Lining up edge, centers, and parallels, trim four corners. S.O.S.

Now you have completed one Pineapple block. When making several blocks, S.O.S. for each row in all blocks. This will help ensure that blocks fit together and will be your key to success. You can chain stitch when making multiple blocks. Chain Row 1 onto one side for all blocks. Cut threads between individual blocks. Chain Row 1 onto opposite side, again for all blocks. Repeat for other two sides. Press blocks and then trim all corners. Continue to chain stitch for each row. Chain stitching saves time, thread, and energy, because you are not getting up and down to press and trim.

Gallery of Quilts

English Cottage Garden *by Linda Nolte Evans, 1989, Englewood, Colorado, 52″ x 52″. A hand-appliqued border enhances this lovely quilt.*

Painted Desert *by Sharon West, 1989, Parker, Colorado, 34″ x 34″. A unique combination of colors creates this traditional Pineapple quilt.*

Watching *by Mary Jo Dalrymple, c. 1984, Little Rock, Arkansas, 50″ x 56″. An exciting use of fabrics creates a strong graphic impact.*

Medusa Project II *by Mary Jo Dalrymple, c. 1983, Little Rock, Arkansas, 52″ x 58″. An unusual interpretation of a traditional design incorporates high contrast with distinctive fabrics.*

Log Cabin Pineapple, *maker unknown, c. 1900, Pennsylvania, 73″ x 78″. An Amish color scheme, punctuated with sharply contrasting lights, gives a continual feeling of movement. (Collection of Bryce and Donna Hamilton)*

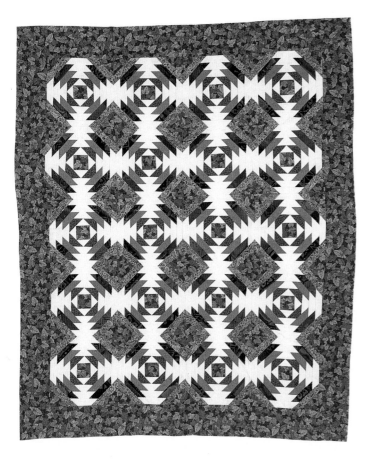

Rhapsody in Blue *by Joanne Malone, 1989, Aurora, Colorado, 44″ x 54″. The bold color scheme of purples and blues combined with stark white inspired this quilt from start to finish.*

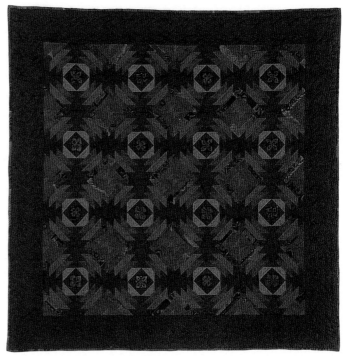

Passion Flower *by Terri Wiley, 1989, Aurora, Colorado, 50″ x 50″. Subtle contrast and intense colors produce a strong visual image.*

Pineapple *by Elizabeth Wright Sherman, c. 1910, Illinois, 81″ x 87″. This beautiful example of an excellently pieced Pineapple quilt displays a wonderful array of scraps. (Collection of Sandra N. Wolf)*

Pineapple *by Charlotte Ballard, 1988, Little Rock, Arkansas, 90″ x 90″. This planned scrap quilt uses a wide variety of brown and rust prints. (Collection of Lynda Milligan and Nancy Smith)*

Mirrors of Autumn by Shirley Sanden, 1988, Wheatridge, Colorado, 40″ x 40″. A traditional interpretation of fall inspired this color palette.

Ojos de Dios by Christine Scott, 1989, Parker, Colorado, 40″ x 40″. Worked from a planned graph, this quilt uses basic solid colors for a southwestern design.

Night Mist by Sharon Holmes, 1989, Lakewood, Colorado, 46″ x 46″. The subtle floral fabric serves as the "light" in this quilt. A companion quilt might use the same fabric as a "medium."

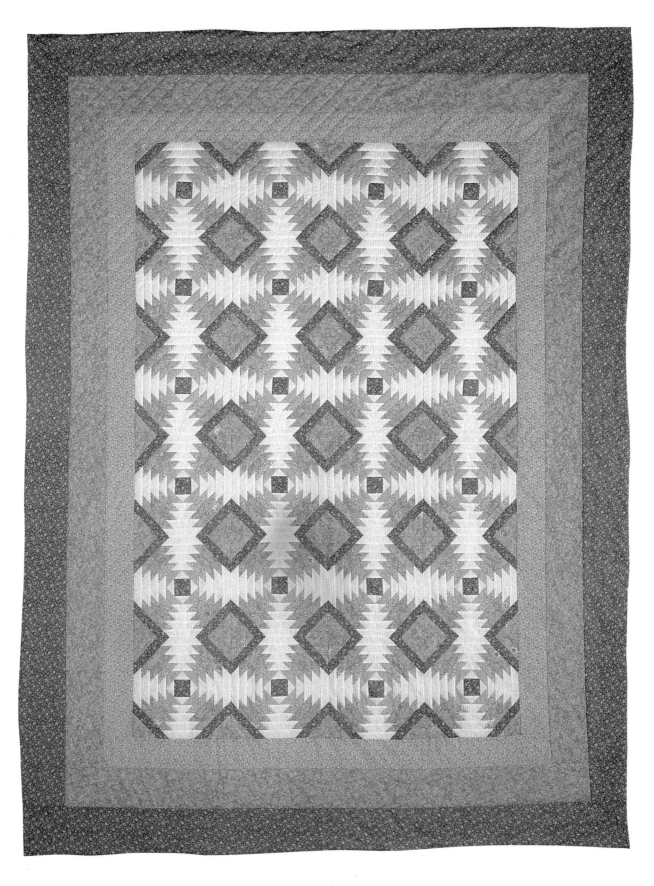

Peaches and Cream *by Janice Hagan, 1989, Aurora, Colorado, 72″ x 90″. A warm and soft color combination becomes a soothing focal point in a bedroom.*

Pineapple *(origin unknown), 70″ x 80″. An appealing combination of fabrics distinguishes this antique quilt. (Collection of Sandy Pape, Cedarburg, Wisconsin)*

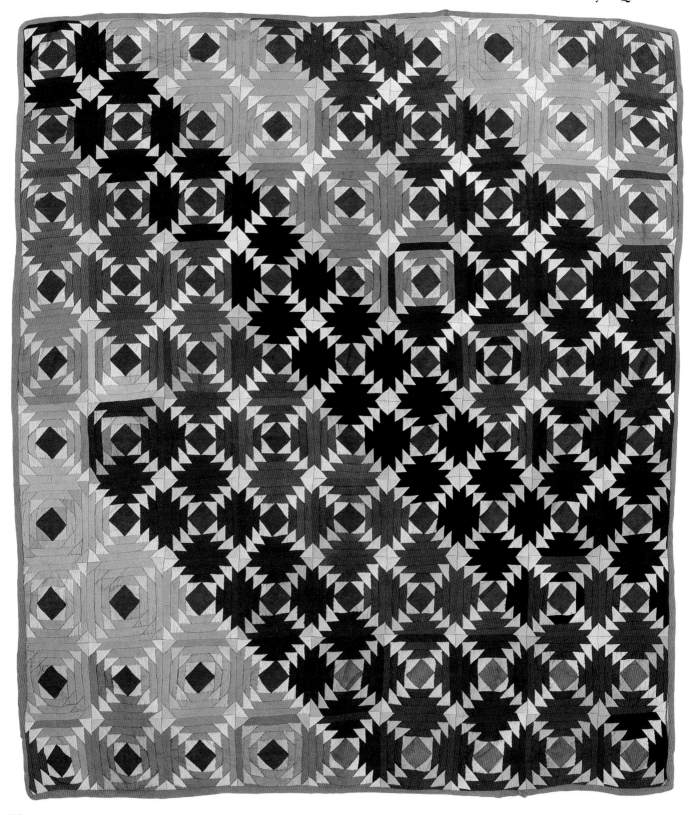

Pineapple *(origin unknown), 60″ x 53″. This antique quilt suggests an almost contemporary color arrangement. (Collection of Luella Doss, Grafton, Wisconsin)*

Pineapple Quilt Patterns

You are ready to begin any of the following quilt patterns. Study the diagrams to see how the colors are arranged. Yardages are generally figured to use the fabric to its best advantage. If you plan on any changes, be sure to buy extra fabric. Cut sizes for all pieces include ¼" seam allowances. For example, if center squares are cut 2½", they will finish to 2"; if logs are cut 1½", they will finish to 1". Borders are generally cut crosswise, unless using a stripe. Measurements for cutting border fabric include extra yardage for mitering corners where needed. Backings may be pieced horizontally for less fabric waste. Yardages include extra fabric to allow for shrinkage.

THIRTY-ONE FLAVORS

Dimensions: Approximately 57" x 68"
10⅞" block

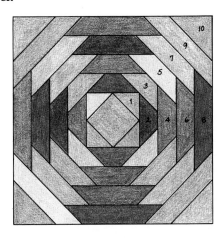

Materials: (44"–45" wide fabric)
3¼ yds. assorted pastel prints for center squares and blocks
1⅞ yds. assorted brown and navy fabric (predominantly brown) for blocks
2⅛ yds. brown stripe for border (if not using stripe, 1½ yds.)
⅝ yd. dark brown print for binding
3½ yds. fabric for backing, pieced horizontally
72" x 90" batting

Cutting

Assorted pastel prints

Center squares	20	2½" x 2½"
Row 1	80 logs	1½" x 2½"
Row 3	80 logs	1½" x 4"
Row 5	80 logs	1½" x 5"
Row 7	80 logs	1½" x 6"
Row 9	80 logs	1½" x 7"
Row 10	80 logs	3" x 5"

Assorted brown and navy fabric

Row 2	80 logs	1½" x 3½"
Row 4	80 logs	1½" x 4½"
Row 6	80 logs	1½" x 5½"
Row 8	80 logs	1½" x 6½"

Borders

If using stripe, cut 2 strips on lengthwise grain, 6½" x 60", for top and bottom. Cut 2 strips on lengthwise grain, 6½" x 72", for sides.

If not using stripe, cut 3 strips and piece ends together to make 2 borders, each 6½" x 60", for top and bottom. Cut 4 strips and piece ends together to make 2 borders, each 6½" x 72", for sides.

Binding

Cut 7 strips, each 2½" wide by fabric width.

Directions

1. Following piecing diagram, piece 20 Pineapple blocks.
2. Set blocks together 4 across by 5 down.
3. Sew borders and miter corners (see Glossary of Techniques on pages 71–72).
4. Layer backing, batting, and quilt top; baste.
5. Quilt blocks as shown in diagram. Choose several stripes for quilting the border.
6. Bind with straight strips of fabric (see Glossary of Techniques on page 73).

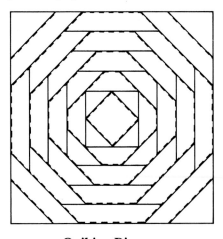

Quilting Diagram

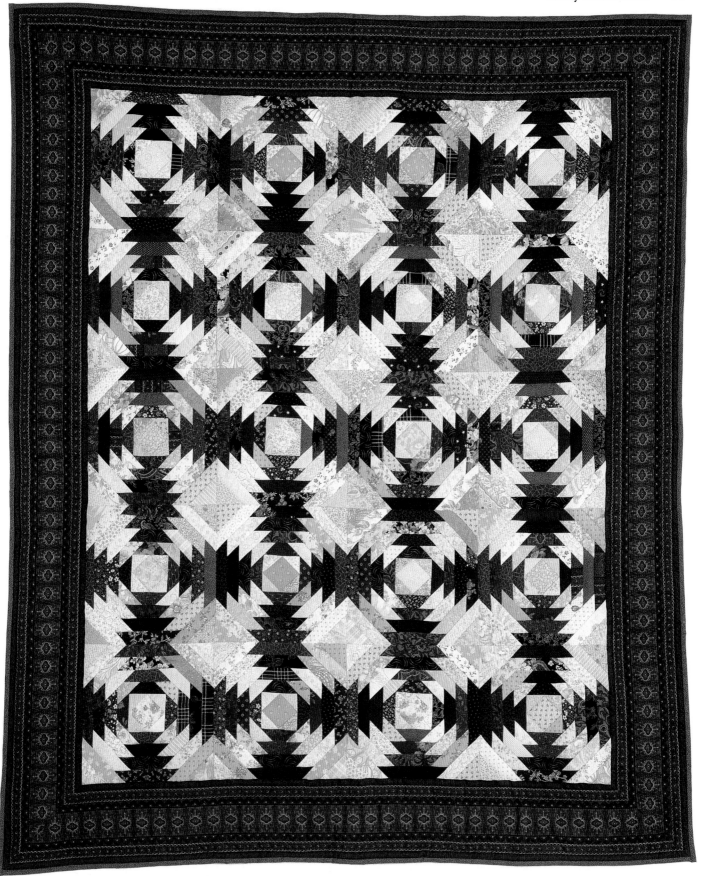

Thirty-One Flavors by Nancy Smith and Lynda Milligan, 1989, Denver, Colorado, 57″ x 68″. The high contrast of the dark browns with the soft pastels emphasizes the spikes of the Pineapple design.

PINE NEEDLES

Dimensions: 71″ x 86″
15″ block

Materials: (44″–45″ wide fabric)
    1¼ yds. large black floral for center squares, row 9, and middle border
    3¼ yds. beige fabric for blocks
    1½ yds. black print A for row 6 and inner border
    2 yds. black print B for row 8 and outer border
    ¾ yd. black print C for row 2
    ⅞ yd. black print D for row 4
    ½ yd. black print E for row 10
    ¾ yd. of one of the prints for binding
    5¼ yds. fabric for backing, pieced vertically
    72″ x 90″ batting

Cutting

Large black floral
Center squares	20	3½″ x 3½″
Row 9	80 logs	2″ x 6″

Beige
Row 1	80 logs	2″ x 3½″
Row 3	80 logs	2″ x 5½″
Row 5	80 logs	2″ x 6½″
Row 7	80 logs	2″ x 8″

Black prints
Row 2	80 logs	2″ x 5½″
Row 4	80 logs	2″ x 6½″
Row 6	80 logs	2″ x 8″
Row 8	80 logs	2″ x 9″
Row 10	80 logs	2″ x 3″

Borders

Inner border (black print)—Cut 4 strips and piece ends together to make 2 borders, each 2″ x 75½″, for sides. Cut 3 strips and piece ends together to make 2 borders, each 2″ x 63½″, for top and bottom.

Middle border (black floral)—Cut 4 strips and piece ends together to make 2 borders, each 1½″ x 78½″, for sides. Cut 4 strips and piece ends together to make 2 borders, each 1½″ x 65½″, for top and bottom.

Outer border (black print)—Cut 4 strips and piece ends together to make 2 borders, each 3½″ x 80½″, for sides. Cut 4 strips and piece ends together to make 2 borders, each 3½″ x 71½″, for top and bottom.

Binding
Cut 8 strips, each 2½″ wide by fabric width.

Directions
1. Following piecing diagram, piece 20 Pineapple blocks.
2. Set blocks 4 across by 5 down.
3. Sew inner border to both sides. Sew inner border to top and bottom.
4. Sew middle border to both sides. Sew middle border to top and bottom.
5. Sew outer border to both sides. Sew outer border to top and bottom.
6. Following diagram, mark quilting design for borders.
7. Layer backing, batting, and quilt top; baste.
8. Quilt blocks as shown in diagram. Quilt borders as marked.
9. Bind with straight strips of fabric (see Glossary of Techniques on page 73).

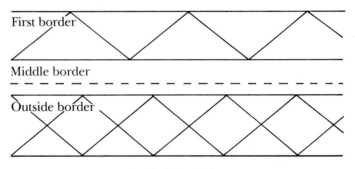

Border Quilting Diagram

Quilting Diagram

Pine Needles *by Nancy Smith and Lynda Milligan, 1989, Denver, Colorado, 71″ x 86″. An overall background print, combined with subtle shades of green and an overall large-scale floral print, suggests the restfulness of a pine forest.*

DOUBLE BUBBLE

Dimensions: 45″ x 57″
12″ block

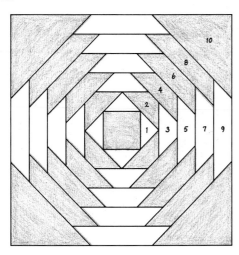

Materials: (44″–45″ wide fabric)
    1½ yds. pink stripe for center squares and inner border
    2¾ yds. pink print for blocks and outer border
    1¼ yds. cream fabric for blocks
    ⅜ yd. pink print for binding
    2¾ yds. fabric for backing, pieced horizontally
    45″ x 60″ batting

Cutting

Pink stripe
Center squares	12	2½″ x 2½″

Pink print
Row 2	48 logs	1½″ x 3½″
Row 4	48 logs	1½″ x 4½″
Row 6	48 logs	1½″ x 5½″
Row 8	48 logs	1½″ x 6½″
Row 10	48 logs	4½″ x 7″

Cream
Row 1	48 logs	1½″ x 2½″
Row 3	48 logs	1½″ x 4″
Row 5	48 logs	1½″ x 5″
Row 7	48 logs	1½″ x 6″
Row 9	48 logs	1½″ x 7″

Borders
    Inner border (pink stripe)—Cut 2 strips on lengthwise grain, 1½″ x 51½″, for sides; cut 3 strips on horizontal grain and piece ends together to make 2 borders, each 1½″ x 36½″, for top and bottom.
    Outer border (pink print)—Cut 2 strips, each 3½″ x 39½″; cut 3 strips and piece ends together to make 2 borders, each 3½″ x 57½″.

Binding
    Cut 5 strips, each 2½″ by fabric width.

Directions
1. Following piecing diagram, piece 12 Pineapple blocks.
2. Set blocks together 3 across by 4 down. Be sure to set blocks with center stripe consistently vertical.
3. Piece the striped border so that the lines of the stripe remain vertical to follow the center squares of Pineapple blocks.
4. Sew striped borders to top and bottom first; then sew striped borders to sides.
5. Sew the print borders to quilt; start with top and bottom, and then sew sides.
6. Using the quilting diagram found on page 77, mark quilt top lightly with a pencil or chalk liner.
7. Layer backing, batting, and quilt top; baste.
8. Following marked design, quilt center of top. Quilt both borders by outline stitching ¼″ from both sides of seams.
9. Bind with straight strips of fabric (see Glossary of Techniques on page 73).

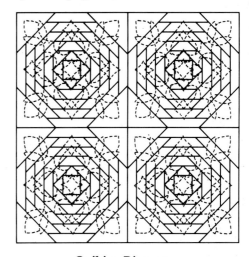

Quilting Diagram

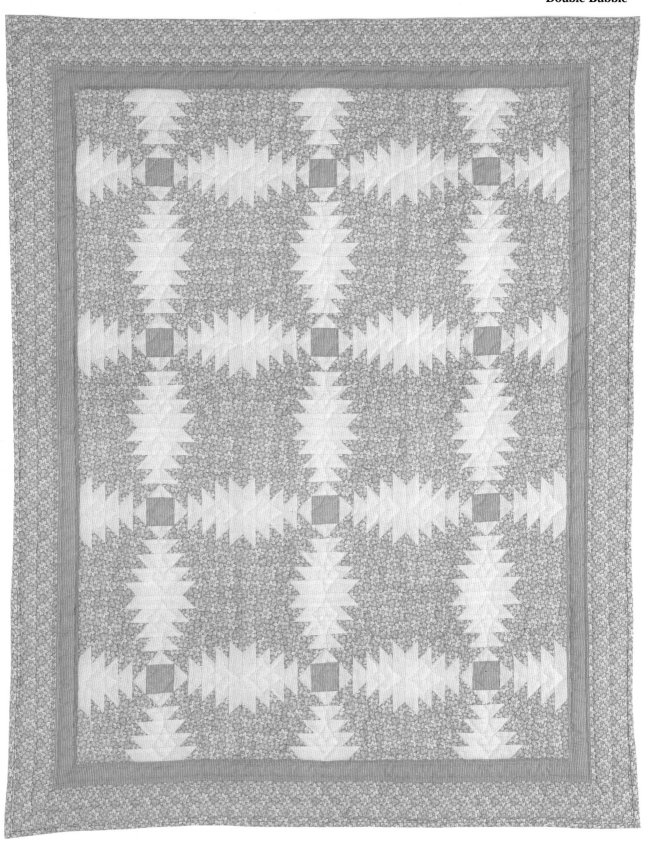

Double Bubble *by Lynda Milligan and Nancy Smith, 1989, Denver, Colorado, 45″ x 57″. An unusual quilting design enhances the simplicity of the soft pinks. Notice the stripe on the border.*

GLAD TIDINGS

Dimensions: 68″ x 68″
15″ block

Materials: (44″–45″ wide fabric)
⅛ yd. red fabric A for center squares
1½ yds. red fabric B for row 4, row 9, and inner
     border
⅜ yd. red fabric C for row 2
½ yd. red fabric D for row 6
½ yd. red fabric E for row 8
1 yd. green fabric A for center squares, row 4, and
     row 9
⅜ yd. green fabric B for row 2
½ yd. green fabric C for row 6
1¼ yds. green fabric D for row 8 and outer border
3¼ yds. cream fabric for blocks
⅝ yd. green print for binding
4¼ yds. fabric for backing
72″ x 90″ batting

Cutting

Reds and greens

Center squares	32 each	2″ x 2″
Row 2	32 logs each	2″ x 5½″
Row 4	32 logs each	2″ x 6½″
Row 6	32 logs each	2″ x 8″
Row 8	32 logs each	2″ x 9″
Row 9	32 logs each	3½″ x 4″

Cream

Row 1	64 logs	2″ x 3½″
Row 3	64 logs	2″ x 5½″
Row 5	64 logs	2″ x 6½″
Row 7	64 logs	2″ x 8″
Row 9	64 logs	3½″ x 4″

Borders

Inner border (red)—Cut 7 strips and piece ends together to make 4 borders, each 2″ x 72″.

Outer border (green)—Cut 7 strips and piece ends together to make 4 borders, each 3″ x 72″.

Binding

Cut 7 strips, each 2½″ by fabric width.

Directions

1. Make 16 Four-Patch red and green center squares.
2. Piece 16 Pineapple blocks, stopping after row 8.
3. For corners, sew 32 red logs to 32 cream logs on the 4″ edge, making a 3½″ x 7½″ rectangle. Sew 32 green logs to 32 cream logs on the 4″ edge, making a 3½″ x 7½″ rectangle.
4. Mark the center point of each log 8. **Hint:** Fold log in half and finger press the center.
5. Match the center point of red log 8 to seam line of green/cream log and pin. Check quilt photo to see if green will be in correct position. If not, flip rectangle around. Sew; repeat 31 times.
6. Match the center point of green log 8 to seam line of red/cream rectangular corner units (see photo for correct placement). Sew; repeat 31 times.
7. Set blocks 4 across by 4 down. Arrange blocks so that the red/cream and green/cream pinwheels form in the corners.
8. Sew the border strips together to make 4 border units, each 4½″ x 72″.
9. Sew borders to quilt and miter corners (see Glossary of Techniques on pages 71–72).
10. Mark quilting design for borders.
11. Layer backing, batting, and quilt top; baste.
12. Quilt blocks as shown in diagram. Quilt borders as marked.
13. Bind with straight strips of fabric (see Glossary of Techniques on page 73).

Quilting Diagram

Glad Tidings *by Nancy Smith and Lynda Milligan, 1989, Denver, Colorado, 68" x 68". The corners of these Pineapple blocks form pinwheels of color. The center Four Patches top the trees of red and green.*

MOSAIC

Dimensions: Approximately 44½″ x 44½″
8⅞″ block

Materials: (44″–45″ wide fabric)
½ yd. dark red for center squares, row 8, and inner border

1½ yds. red print for blocks and outer border
1¾ yds. black print for blocks and middle border
⅜ yd. dark red for binding
1⅝ yds. fabric for backing
45″ x 60″ batting

Cutting

Dark red
Center squares	16	2½″ x 2½″
Row 8	64 logs	¾″ x 3″

Red print
Row 2	64 logs	1½″ x 3½″
Row 4	64 logs	1½″ x 4½″
Row 6	64 logs	1½″ x 5½″

Black print
Row 1	64 logs	1½″ x 2½″
Row 3	64 logs	1½″ x 4″
Row 5	64 logs	1½″ x 5″
Row 7	64 logs	1½″ x 6″
Row 9	64 logs	1½″ x 2½″

Borders

Inner border (dark red)—Cut 5 strips and piece ends together to make 4 borders, each ¾″ x 47″.

Middle border (black print)—Cut 5 strips and piece ends together to make 4 borders, each 2″ x 47″.

Outer border (red print)—Cut 5 strips and piece ends together to make 4 borders, each 3″ x 47″.

Binding

Cut 5 strips, each 2½″ by fabric width.

Directions

1. Following piecing diagram, piece together 16 Pineapple blocks. **Note:** Log 8 finishes to a ¼″ strip.
2. Set blocks 4 across by 4 down.
3. Sew the border strips together to make 4 border units, each 47″ long.
4. Sew borders to quilt and miter corners (see Glossary of Techniques on pages 71–72).
5. Mark quilting design as shown in diagram.
6. Layer backing, batting, and quilt top; baste.
7. Quilt as desired.
8. Bind with straight strips of fabric (see Glossary of Techniques on page 73).

Quilting Diagram

Mosaic *by Kathy Simes, 1989, Aurora, Colorado, 44½″ x 44½″. Color and print choice create a definite Oriental influence. Notice the variation of log size.*

KIMBERLY'S KALEIDOSCOPE

Dimensions: 70″ x 100″
15″ block

Materials: (44″–45″ wide fabric)
    6 yds. assorted dark prints for center squares,
       blocks, and pieced squares
    4 yds. assorted light prints (most with beige
       background) for blocks
    1¼ yds. blue for inner and outer borders
    ¾ yd. blue for binding
    6 yds. fabric for backing
    90″ x 108″ batting

Cutting

Assorted dark prints

Center squares	24	3½″ x 3½″
Row 2	96 logs	2″ x 5½″
Row 4	96 logs	2″ x 6½″
Row 6	96 logs	2″ x 8″
Row 8	96 logs	2″ x 9″
Row 9	96 logs	2″ x 6″
Row 10	96 logs	2″ x 3″

Assorted light prints

Row 1	96 logs	2″ x 3½″
Row 3	96 logs	2″ x 5½″
Row 5	96 logs	2″ x 6½″
Row 7	96 logs	2″ x 8″

Borders

    Inner and outer borders (blue)—Cut 8 strips and piece ends together to make 4 borders (2 for top and 2 for bottom), each 2¼″ x 75″. Cut 10 strips and piece ends together to make 4 borders (2 for each side), each 2¼″ x 105″.

    Pieced squares (assorted dark prints)—Cut approximately 242 squares 2″ x 2″.

Binding

    Cut 9 strips, each 2½″ by fabric width.

Directions

1. Following the piecing diagram, piece 24 Pineapple blocks.
2. Set blocks 4 across by 6 down.
3. Piece 2″ squares together into 2 strips, approximately 75½″ long, and 2 strips, approximately 105½″ long.
4. Sew blue border strips to either side of pieced strips.
5. Following mitering directions, sew completed borders to quilt top. Try to match squares at corners (see Glossary of Techniques on pages 71–72).
6. Layer backing, batting, and quilt top; baste.
7. Outline quilt ¼″ from each seam.
8. Bind with straight strips of fabric (see Glossary of Techniques on page 73).

Quilting Diagram

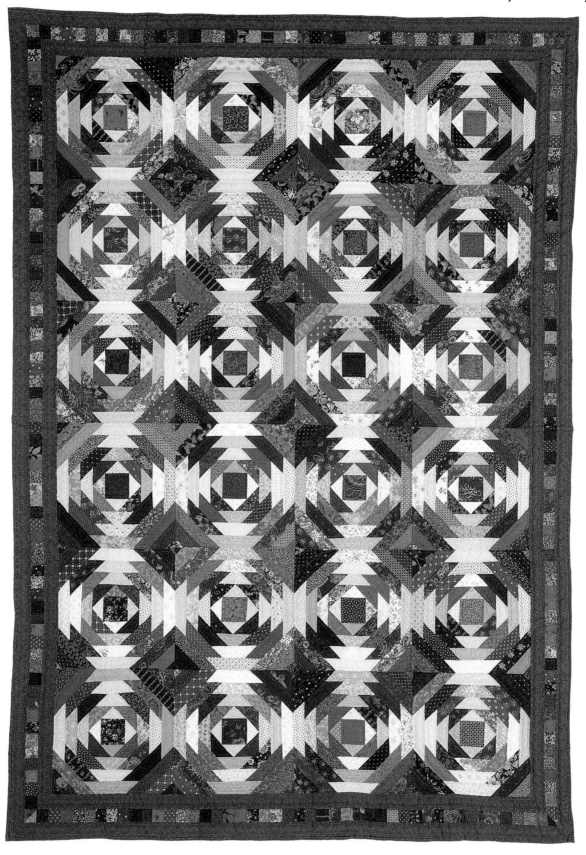

Kimberly's Kaleidoscope *by Lynda Milligan and Nancy Smith, 1989, Denver, Colorado, 70″ x 100″. Scraps of fabric left over from another project combine with assorted beige background prints to create this warm quilt.*

INTERLAKEN

Dimensions: Approximately 51″ x 75″
12″ block

Materials: (44″–45″ wide fabric)
3 yds. dark brown floral for center squares, blocks, pieced and outer borders
1¾ yds. gold for blocks and pieced border
⅜ yd. red for inner and pieced border
½ yd. dark brown for binding
3¼ yds. fabric for backing, pieced horizontally
72″ x 90″ batting

Cutting

Dark brown

Center squares	15	3½″ x 3½″

(Center flower in each square.)

Row 2	60 logs	2″ x 3½″
Row 4	60 logs	2″ x 4½″
Row 6	60 logs	2″ x 5½″
Row 7	60 logs	3″ x 4½″

Gold

Row 1	60 logs	2″ x 2½″
Row 3	60 logs	2″ x 4″
Row 5	60 logs	2″ x 5″

Borders

Inner border (red)—Cut 2 strips, each 2″ x 40½″; cut 3 strips and piece ends together to make 2 borders, each 2″ x 52½″.

Pieced border—Cut 48 dark brown floral 2⅞″ squares in half to make 96 triangles, cut 48 gold 2⅞″ squares in half to make 96 triangles, and cut 1 red strip 2½″ by fabric width.

Outer border (dark brown floral)—Cut 3 strips and piece ends together to make 2 borders, each 4½″ x 53½″; cut 3 strips and piece ends together to make 2 borders, each 4½″ x 65½″.

Binding

Cut 6 strips, each 2½″ by fabric width.

Directions

1. Following piecing diagram, piece 15 Pineapple blocks.
2. Set blocks together 3 across by 5 down.
3. Sew inner red borders to top and bottom of quilt. Sew inner red borders to sides of quilt. Following directions in Glossary of Techniques on pages 71–72, miter corners.
4. Following quilt photo, piece triangles together for pieced border. Side borders consist of 30 sets of triangles; top and bottom borders consist of 18 sets. Add a red 2″ strip to each end to finish out strip length. Allow a little extra for mitering. Stitch to quilt, stopping ¼″ from strip edge.
5. Sew dark brown floral outer borders to top and bottom of quilt, stopping ¼″ from strip edge. Sew dark brown floral outer borders to sides of quilt. Miter last 2 borders together.
6. Layer backing, batting, and quilt top; baste.
7. Quilt as desired. We have outline quilted all blocks and the pieced border. A small cable is quilted in the red strip, with a heart at the corner and a floral design in the brown border.
8. Bind with straight strips of fabric (see Glossary of Techniques on page 73).

Quilting Diagram

Interlaken *by Ruth Haggbloom, 1989, Denver, Colorado, 51" x 75". A different direction in color and the excitement of a new technique inspired this artist. Interlaken was the name of her grandparent's resort, and the deep colors recalled lovely fall memories.*

VICTORIANA

Dimensions: Approximately 35″ x 35″
14⅞″ block

↖ Center of quilt

Materials: (44″–45″ wide fabric)
- ¼ yd. each light peach, blue, and green for center squares, blocks, and pieced border
- ¼ yd. each medium peach, blue, and green for blocks and pieced border
- 1 yd. black floral for blocks and pieced border
- ¾ yd. black solid for blocks and borders
- 1¼ yds. fabric for backing
- ½ yd. black solid for binding
- 45″ x 60″ batting

Cutting

Light peach

Center squares	4	2½″ x 2½″
Row 6	8 logs	1½″ x 5½″
Row 15	4 logs	1½″ x 4″

Light blue

Row 2	8 logs	1½″ x 3½″

Light green

Row 4	8 logs	1½″ x 4½″

Medium peach

Row 12	8 logs	1½″ x 8½″

Medium blue

Row 8	8 logs	1½″ x 6½″

Medium green

Row 10	8 logs	1½″ x 7½″

Black floral

Row 1	12 logs	1½″ x 2½″
Row 3	12 logs	1½″ x 4″
Row 5	12 logs	1½″ x 5″
Row 7	12 logs	1½″ x 6″
Row 9	12 logs	1½″ x 7″
Row 11	12 logs	1½″ x 8″
Row 13	12 logs	1½″ x 9″
Row Y	4 logs	1½″ x 9″
Row 14	12 logs	1½″ x 7″
Row 15	12 logs	1½″ x 5″

Black solid

Row 2	8 logs	1½″ x 3½″
Row 4	8 logs	1½″ x 4½″
Row 6	8 logs	1½″ x 5½″
Row 8	8 logs	1½″ x 6½″
Row 10	8 logs	1½″ x 7½″
Row 12	8 logs	1½″ x 8½″
Row 1	4 logs	1½″ x 2½″
Row 3	4 logs	1½″ x 4″
Row 5	4 logs	1½″ x 5″
Row 7	4 logs	1½″ x 6″
Row 9	4 logs	1½″ x 7″
Row 11	4 logs	1½″ x 8″
Row X	4 logs	1″ x 8″
Row Z	4 logs	1″ x 5″

Borders

Inner border (black solid)—Cut 4 strips, each 1¼″ x 38″.

Pieced border—Cut one 4½″ by fabric width strip of large black floral and cut one 1″ by fabric width strip of each light and medium solid, plus 2 black solid strips.

Binding

Cut 4 strips, each 3½″ by fabric width.

Directions

1. Following piecing diagram, piece 4 Pineapple blocks through Row 11.
2. Note that 3 corners of each block follow the normal Pineapple piecing procedure. The fourth corner is pieced in the same manner, but log X is narrower than the adjacent logs. This will offset that corner, and log Z will complete the 1″ strip measurement. (Strips X and Z together make up the total measurement for a "regular" strip.)
3. For the pieced border, sew the solid strips together with a black strip on either end. Using the 45° angle from the Pineapple Rule, begin cutting sections of color. Cut 8 sections 1½″ wide and then cut from the other end of the pieced strip, so that sections are reversed. Cut 8 more sections. Cut 1½″ strips from the floral fabric also. Piece together, following the photo of the quilt. Notice that the extra black strip is removed at the corners. If the measurement needs to

be adjusted, adjust the width of the black floral strip.

4. Stitch the black inner border onto the pieced strips.
5. Sew to quilt, mitering the corners (see Glossary of Techniques on pages 71–72).
6. Layer backing, batting, and quilt top; baste.
7. Following diagram, quilt.
8. Bind with straight strips of fabric (see Glossary of Techniques on page 73). Note that these strips are extra wide so that the binding finishes the same width as the inner border.

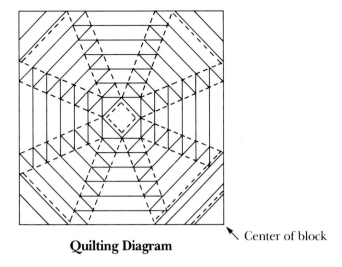

↖ Center of block

Quilting Diagram

Victoriana by Sharon Holmes, 1989, Lakewood, Colorado, 35" x 35". The use of black with pastels has a dramatic effect. The quilt appears to be more complex than it is—all four blocks are identical.

LILY PAD

Dimensions: 58″ x 58″
10″ block

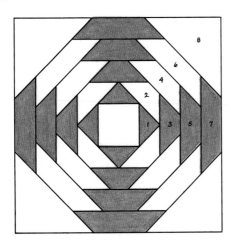

Materials: (44″–45″ wide fabric)
3¼ yds. white print for center squares and blocks
2¼ yds. green stripe for blocks
⅜ yd. peach for inner border
¼ yd. blue for middle border
⅝ yd. green for outer border
3¾ yds. fabric for backing
½ yd. green print for binding
72″ x 90″ batting

Cutting

White print

Center squares	25	2½″ x 2½″
Row 2	100 logs	1½″ x 3½″
Row 4	100 logs	1½″ x 4½″
Row 6	100 logs	1½″ x 5½″
Row 8	100 logs	3½″ x 6½″

Green stripe

Row 1	100 logs	1½″ x 2½″
Row 3	100 logs	1½″ x 4″
Row 5	100 logs	1½″ x 5″
Row 7	100 logs	1½″ x 6″

Borders

Inner border (peach)—Cut 6 strips and piece ends together to make 4 borders, each 1¾″ x 62″.

Middle border (blue)—Cut 6 strips and piece ends together to make 4 borders, each 1¼″ x 62″.

Outer border (green)—Cut 6 strips and piece ends together to make 4 borders, each 3″ x 62″.

Binding

Cut 6 strips, each 2½″ by width of fabric.

Directions

1. Following piecing diagram, piece 25 Pineapple blocks.
2. Set blocks 5 across by 5 down.
3. Sew the border strips together to make 4 border units (top, bottom, sides), each 5″ x 62″.
4. Sew borders to quilt; miter corners (see Glossary of Techniques on pages 71–72).
5. Layer backing, batting, and quilt top; baste.
6. Following diagram, machine or hand quilt.
7. Bind with straight strips of fabric (see Glossary of Techniques on page 73).

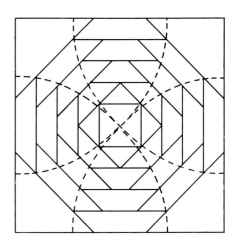

Quilting Diagram

Lily Pad *by Nancy Smith and Lynda Milligan, 1989, Denver, Colorado, 58″ x 58″. A small pond filled with lily pads was the inspiration for this title. One can almost see the ripples created by the Pineapple block with the circular quilt design.*

TAPESTRY

Dimensions: 60″ x 60″
12″ block

Materials: (44″–45″ wide fabric)
  1½ yds. assorted blue prints for center squares
    and blocks
  1⅛ yds. assorted red prints for blocks
  1⅛ yds. assorted yellow prints for blocks
  1½ yds. assorted green prints for blocks
  1¼ yds. green print for border
  ½ yd. green solid for binding
  3⅝ yds. fabric for backing
  72″ x 90″ batting

Cutting
Blue
Center squares   16   2½″ x 2½″

Red and yellow
Row 1   32 logs each   1½″ x 2½″
Row 3   32 logs each   1½″ x 4″
Row 5   32 logs each   1½″ x 5″
Row 7   32 logs each   1½″ x 6″
Row 9   32 logs each   1½″ x 7″

Green and blue
Row 2   32 logs each   1½″ x 3½″
Row 4   32 logs each   1½″ x 4½″
Row 6   32 logs each   1½″ x 5½″
Row 8   32 logs each   1½″ x 6½″
Row 10   32 logs each   4″ x 7½″

Borders
  Cut 3 strips and piece ends together to make 2
borders, each 6½″ x 48½″. Cut 3 strips and piece ends
together to make 2 borders, each 6½″ x 60½″.

Binding
  Cut 6 strips, each 2½″ by fabric width.

Directions
1. Piece 16 Pineapple blocks. **Note:** The red logs must always remain to the right side of the blue logs.
2. Set blocks 4 across by 4 down.
3. Sew wide green borders to top and bottom of quilt.
4. Sew wide green borders to sides of quilt.
5. Mark quilting design as shown in diagram.
6. Layer backing, batting, and quilt top; baste.
7. Quilt blocks and borders.
8. Bind with straight strips of fabric (see Glossary of Techniques on page 73).

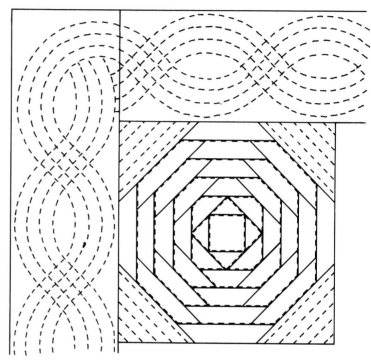

Quilting Diagram

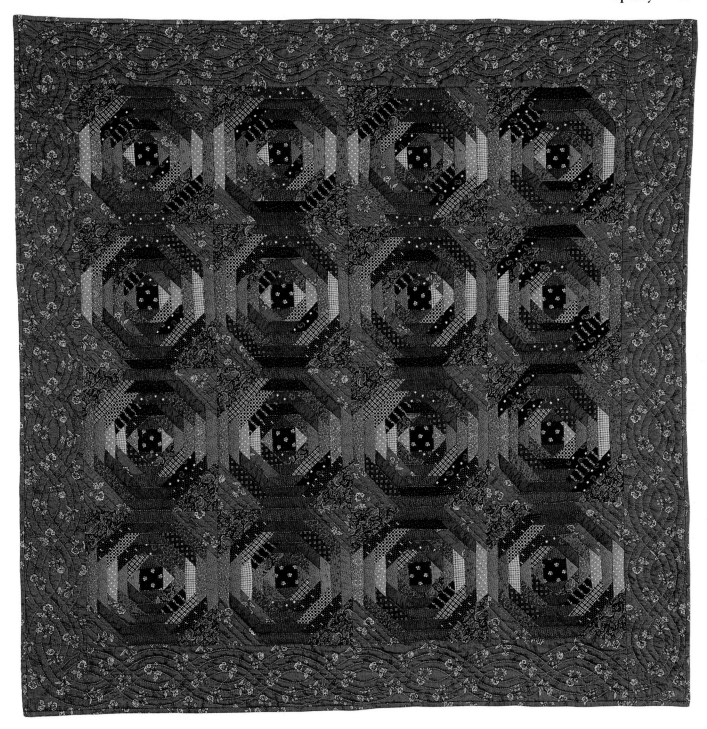

Tapestry *by Nancy Martin, 1989, Woodinville, Washington, 60" x 60". Color bands running diagonally, vertically, and horizontally catch the eye, while the scraps provide variation within this color recipe.*

BLUE WILLOW

Dimensions: 49″ x 64″
15″ block

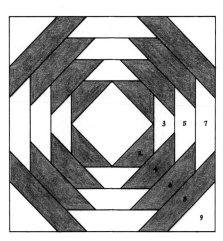

Materials: (44″–45″ wide fabric)
   3 yds. white for center squares, blocks, and border
   2 yds. navy blue for blocks
   ½ yd. navy for binding
   3⅛ yds. fabric for backing, pieced horizontally
   72″ x 90″ batting

Cutting
White
Center squares   12   6½″ x 6½″
(Center squares are longer because they
include Row 1.)

Row 3	48 logs	2″ x 5½″
Row 5	48 logs	2″ x 6½″
Row 7	48 logs	2″ x 8″
Row 9	48 logs	3½″ x 6″

Navy

Row 2	48 logs	2″ x 5½″
Row 4	48 logs	2″ x 6½″
Row 6	48 logs	2″ x 8″
Row 8	48 logs	2″ x 9″

Borders
   Cut 3 strips from white and piece ends together to
make 2 borders, each 2½″ x 45½″, for top and bottom.
Cut 3 strips from white and piece ends together to make
2 borders, each 2½″ x 63½″, for sides.

Binding
   Cut 6 strips, each 2½″ by fabric width.

Directions
1. Following piecing diagram, piece 12 Pineapple blocks.
2. Set blocks 3 across by 4 down.
3. Sew borders to top and bottom of quilt; sew borders to sides of quilt.
4. Mark quilting design as shown in diagram.
5. Layer backing, batting, and quilt top; baste.
6. Quilt blocks. Quilt borders ¼″ from each side seam.
7. Bind with straight strips of fabric (see Glossary of Techniques on page 73).

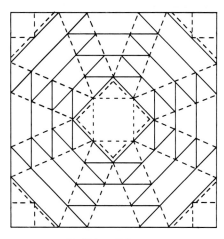

Quilting Diagram

Blue Willow by Nancy Smith and Lynda Milligan, 1989, Denver, Colorado, 49″ x 64″. *The angularity of this blue-and-white quilt is softened by the unusual quilting design.*

REFLECTIONS

Dimensions: 41″ x 51″
10″ block

Materials: (44″–45″ wide fabric)
    ⅛ yd. gold lamé for center squares
    1⅛ yds. lavender watercolor fabric for blocks
    2 yds. black floral for blocks and outer border
    1⅝ yds. pink stripe for inner border (if not using a
        stripe, ⅜ yd.)
    ⅜ yd. black-and-white print for middle border
    ⅜ yd. black floral for binding
    1⅝ yds. fabric for backing
    45″ x 60″ batting

Cutting

Gold lamé

Center squares	12	2½″ x 2½″

Lavender watercolor

Row 1	48 logs	1½″ x 2½″
Row 3	48 logs	1½″ x 4″
Row 5	48 logs	1½″ x 5″
Row 7	48 logs	1½″ x 6″

Black floral

Row 2	48 logs	1½″ x 3½″
Row 4	48 logs	1½″ x 4½″
Row 6	48 logs	1½″ x 5½″
Row 8	48 logs	3½″ x 6½″

Borders

Inner border (pink stripe)—Cut 3 strips on lengthwise grain and piece ends together to make 2 borders, each 1½″ x 55″; cut 2 strips, each 1½″ x 44″, on lengthwise grain. If not using stripe, cut strips on crosswise grain and piece ends together as above.

Middle border (black-and-white print)—Cut 3 strips and piece ends together to make 2 borders, each 2″ x 55″; cut 2 strips, each 2″ x 44″.

Outer border (black floral)—Cut 3 strips and piece ends together to make 2 borders, each 3½″ x 55″; cut 2 strips, each 3½″ x 44″.

Binding

Cut 5 strips, each 2½″ by fabric width.

Directions

1. Following piecing diagram, piece 12 Pineapple blocks.
2. Set blocks together 3 across by 4 down.
3. Sew the border strips together to make 4 border units.
4. Sew borders to quilt and miter corners (see Glossary of Techniques on pages 71–72).
5. Layer backing, batting, and quilt top; baste.
6. Quilt blocks as shown in diagram. Quilt borders as shown in diagram.
7. Bind with straight strips of fabric (see Glossary of Techniques on page 73).

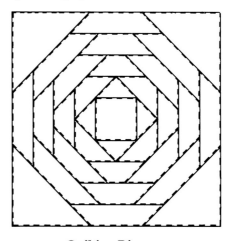

Quilting Diagram

Pink
- - - - - -

Black print
- - - - - - -
- - - - - - -

Black floral

Border Quilting Diagram

Reflections *by Nancy Smith and Lynda Milligan, 1989, Denver, Colorado, 41″ x 51″. An accent touch of lamé gives this quilt a look of enchantment. The traditional Pineapple design is lost, due to the use of the large-scale cotton chintz fabric.*

PINEAPPLE FOLIAGE

Dimensions: 45″ x 45″
15″ block

Quilting Diagram

Materials: (44″–45″ wide fabric)
    2⅛ yds. blue for center squares and blocks
       (if using a stripe, 2½ yds.)
    1½ yds. yellow for blocks
    ⅜ yd. blue for binding
    2¾ yds. fabric for backing
    45″ x 60″ batting

Cutting
    Blue (If using stripe as shown, logs may need to be
       hand cut.)

Center squares	9	3½″ x 3½″
(or use template at right for striped fabric)		
Row 2	36 logs	2″ x 5½″
Row 4	36 logs	2″ x 6½″
Row 6	36 logs	2″ x 8″
Row 8	36 logs	2″ x 9″
Row 9	36 logs	3½″ x 6″

    Yellow

Row 1	36 logs	2″ x 3½″
Row 3	36 logs	2″ x 5½″
Row 5	36 logs	2″ x 6½″
Row 7	36 logs	2″ x 8″

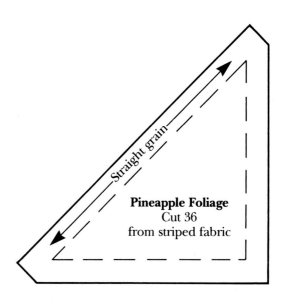

Piece 4 triangles together to make 9 squares.

Binding
    Cut 5 strips, each 2½″ by fabric width.

Directions
1. Following piecing diagram, piece 9 Pineapple blocks.
   If using stripe, be sure to match corners.
2. Set blocks 3 across by 3 down.
3. Layer backing, batting, and quilt top; baste.
4. Quilt blocks as shown in diagram.
5. Bind quilt with straight strips of fabric (see Glossary
   of Techniques on page 73).

Pineapple Foliage *by Opal Homersham, 1989, Aurora, Colorado, 45″ x 45″. The vines of the blue fabric entwine around the rows of logs in this charming quilt. The complementary colors create a fresh feeling.*

MAY NIGHT

Dimensions: 47½″ x 47½″
12″ block

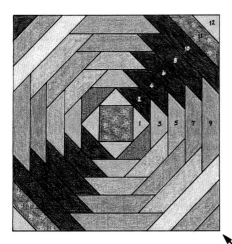

↖ Center of quilt

Materials: (44″–45″ wide fabric)
¼ yd. black (large floral) for center squares and row 11
½ yd. black solid for inner border and blocks
⅛ yd. each of 6 pink prints for middle border and blocks
1½ yds. dark green print for outer border and row 9
⅛ yd. each of 3 green prints for rows 1, 3, and 5
⅙ yd. each of 2 green prints for rows 7 and 12
⅛ yd. black (small floral) for row 12
½ yd. green print for binding
3 yds. fabric for backing
72″ x 90″ batting

Cutting

Black (large floral)

Center squares	4	2½″ x 2½″
Row 11	8 logs	1½″ x 5½″

Black solid

Row 2	8 logs	1½″ x 3½″
Row 4	8 logs	1½″ x 4½″
Row 6	8 logs	1½″ x 5½″
Row 8	8 logs	1½″ x 6½″
Row 10	8 logs	1½″ x 7½″

Pink prints

Row 2	8 logs	1½″ x 3½″
Row 4	8 logs	1½″ x 4½″
Row 6	8 logs	1½″ x 5½″
Row 8	8 logs	1½″ x 6½″
Row 10	8 logs	1½″ x 7½″
Row 11	8 logs	1½″ x 5½″

Dark green

Row 9	16 logs	1½″ x 7½″

Green prints

Row 1	16 logs	1½″ x 3½″
Row 3	16 logs	1½″ x 4½″
Row 5	16 logs	1½″ x 5½″
Row 7	16 logs	1½″ x 6½″
Row 12	8 logs	2″ x 5½″

Black (small floral)

Row 12	8 logs	2″ x 3½″

Borders

Inner border (black solid)—Cut 2 strips 2″ x 24½″; cut 2 strips 2″ x 27½″.

Middle border (pink prints)—Cut 76 squares, 2″ x 2″, of assorted prints and piece together to make 2 borders of 18 squares, each 2″ x 27½″, and 2 borders of 20 squares, each 2″ x 30½″.

Outer border (dark green print)—Cut 2 strips, each 9″ x 30½″; cut 3 strips and piece ends together to make 2 borders, each 9″ x 47½″.

Binding

Cut 5 strips, each 2½″ by fabric width.

Directions

1. Following piecing diagram and photo, piece 4 Pineapple blocks.
2. Set blocks 2 across by 2 down.
3. Sew top and bottom inner border to quilt. Sew inner side borders to quilt.
4. Piece 2″ squares together to make middle borders. Piece together two 2″ x 27½″ borders of squares. Sew to top and bottom of quilt. Piece together two 2″ x 30½″ borders of squares. Sew to sides of quilt.
5. Sew outer border to top and bottom. Sew outer border to sides.
6. Layer backing, batting, and quilt top; baste.
7. Following diagram, quilt. Quilt borders as desired or as shown in photo.
8. Bind with straight strips of fabric (see Glossary of Techniques on page 73).

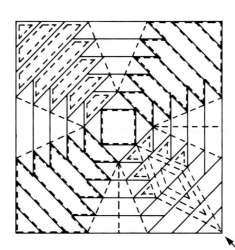

Quilting Diagram

↖ Center of quilt

May Night *by Janet Robinson, 1989, Englewood, Colorado, 47½″ x 47½″. The intricacy of this Pineapple quilt is enhanced by the wonderful quilting designs. Some of these designs are echoed in the border.*

CROCUS

Dimensions: 32″ x 42″
10″ block

Materials: (44″–45″ wide fabric)
½ yd. total of assorted brights (3 shades per block)
    for center squares, blocks, and middle border
1½ yds. black for blocks and inner and outer
    borders
⅛ yd. each of 6 assorted greens for blocks
⅜ yd. black for binding
1 yd. fabric for backing
45″ x 60″ batting

Cutting

Brights

Center squares	6	2½″ x 2½″
Row 1	24 logs	1½″ x 2½″
Row 2	12 logs	1½″ x 3½″
Row 3	12 logs	1½″ x 4″

Black

Row 2	12 logs	1½″ x 3½″
Row 3	6 logs	1½″ x 4″
Row 4	24 logs	1½″ x 4½″
Row 5	18 logs	1½″ x 5″
Row 6	12 logs	1½″ x 5½″
Row 7	18 logs	1½″ x 6″
Row 8	24 logs	3½″ x 6½″

Greens

Row 3	6 logs	1½″ x 4″
Row 5	6 logs	1½″ x 5″
Row 6	12 logs	1½″ x 5½″
Row 7	6 logs	1½″ x 6″

Borders

Inner border (black)—Cut 2 strips, each 2½″ x 30½″, for sides; cut 2 strips, each 2½″ x 24½″, for top and bottom.

Middle border (brights)—Cut approximately 130 squares, each 1½″ x 1½″.

Outer border (black)—Cut 2 strips, each 3½″ x 36½″, for sides; cut 2 strips, each 3½″ x 32½″, for top and bottom.

Binding

Cut 4 strips, each 2½″ by fabric width.

Directions

1. Following piecing diagram, piece 6 Pineapple blocks.
2. Set blocks together 2 across by 3 down.
3. Sew black inner borders to sides of quilt. Sew black inner borders to top and bottom of quilt.
4. Piece 1½″ squares together to fit quilt. Matching squares at corners, sew onto borders.
5. Sew black outer borders to quilt. Sew sides first and then top and bottom.
6. Mark quilting design on borders. Mark center square design on blocks.
7. Layer backing, batting, and quilt top; baste.
8. Following Quilting Diagram, quilt blocks. Quilt borders as marked in Border Quilting Diagram.
9. Bind with straight strips of fabric (see Glossary of Techniques on page 73).

Quilting Diagram

Border Quilting Diagram

***Crocus** by Nancy Smith and Lynda Milligan, 1989, Denver, Colorado, 32" x 42". Color placement gives a new look to a traditional design.*

PINEAPPLE TIDBITS

Dimensions: 74″ x 98″
10″ block

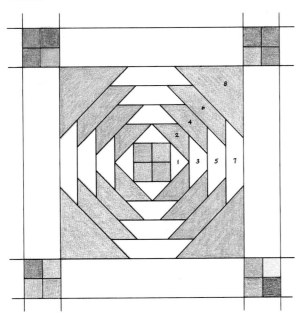

Materials: (44″–45″ wide fabric)
  6 yds. muslin for blocks and setting strips
  ⅛ yd. or 9″ x 18″ piece of each assorted print (up to
    96 different) for blocks
  ¾ yd. muslin for binding
  6 yds. fabric for backing
  90″ x 108″ batting

Cutting

Muslin

Setting strips	110	2½″ x 10½″
Row 1	192 logs	1½″ x 2½″
Row 3	192 logs	1½″ x 4″
Row 5	192 logs	1½″ x 5″
Row 7	192 logs	1½″ x 6″

Print (for each of the 48 blocks)

Small squares	4 each of two colors	1½″ x 1½″
Row 2	2 each of two colors	1½″ x 3½″
Row 4	2 each of two colors	1½″ x 4½″
Row 6	2 each of two colors	1½″ x 5½″
Row 8	2 each of two colors	3½″ x 6½″

Extra small squares	60	1½″ x 1½″

Binding

  Cut 9 strips, each 2½″ by fabric width.

Directions

1. Following piecing diagram, piece 48 Pineapple blocks. Use muslin and 2 different prints for each block.
2. Lay out all blocks 6 across by 8 down.
3. Once you have decided on your final block placement, make the setting strips.
4. Make Row 1 the top crosswise row of setting strips. These rows must be coordinated with your block colors, as they are extensions of the diagonal Pineapple block colors. Where setting squares do not extend from the Pineapple block, as in the corners and outside edges, choose any of the various prints to complete the square. Following diagram and color photo, make 8 more rows.

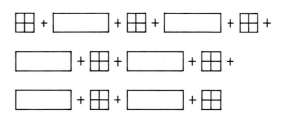

5. Sew 8 crosswise rows of Pineapple blocks together, beginning and ending with a setting strip.
6. Sew Row 1 of setting strips to Row 1 of blocks and continue to assemble quilt, following diagram.
7. Mark quilting design, as shown in diagram.
8. Layer backing, batting, and quilt top; baste.
9. Quilt blocks and setting strips.
10. Bind with straight strips of fabric (see Glossary of Techniques on page 73).

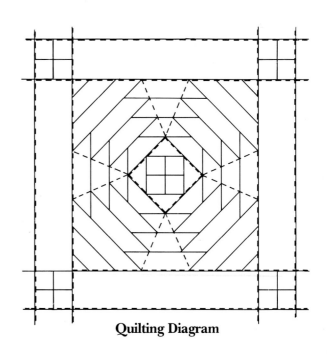

Quilting Diagram

Pineapple Tidbits *by Nancy Smith and Lynda Milligan, 1989, Denver, Colorado, 74″ x 98″. Strips of muslin, the background color of the blocks, are used to set this quilt together. The setting squares repeat the Pineapple centers. The variety of pastel scraps creates a "summer fruit salad."*

PLACE MATS

Dimensions: Approximately 14″ x 18″

Materials: (44″–45″ wide fabric)
(for a set of 4 place mats)
⅞ yd. large floral print for center squares and
    rows 4, 6, and 7
¼ yd. small floral for row 2
½ yd. beige scales for rows 1 and 5
¼ yd. beige squiggles for row 3
⅝ yd. large floral print for binding
1 yd. fabric for backing
1 yd. needlepunch
Matching thread for backing fabric

Cutting

Large floral

Center squares	4	3½″ x 3½″
Row 4	16 logs	2½″ x 6½″
Row 6	16 logs	2½″ x 8½″
Row 7	8 logs	2½″ x 10½″

Small floral

Row 2	16 logs	2½″ x 5″

Beige scales

Row 1	16 logs	2½″ x 3½″
Row 5	16 logs	2½″ x 8½″

Beige squiggles

Row 3	16 logs	2½″ x 7″

Binding

Cut 7 strips, each 2½″ by fabric width.

Directions

1. These place mats use "quilt-as-you-go" techniques, so be sure to measure on the right side of the fabric. Cut 4 rectangles 16″ x 20″ from backing fabric.
2. Cut 4 rectangles 16″ x 20″ from needlepunch.
3. For each place mat, layer backing, wrong side up, and needlepunch.
4. With a pencil, draw diagonal lines on the needlepunch from corner to corner.

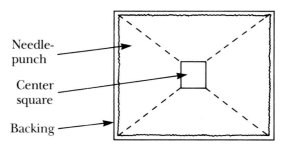

5. Lay center square on needlepunch center (where diagonal lines cross), matching corners of square to diagonal lines. Pin in place.
6. Wind bobbin with thread that matches backing fabric.
7. With right sides together and raw edges even, sew logs of Row 1 to top and bottom of center square. Sew through backing and needlepunch. Finger press logs toward the outside edges. Repeat for sides. Press logs toward outside edges. Check backing before and after every row to make sure you are not sewing in pleats.
8. Line up Pineapple Rule as shown in step 5 on page 22. Mark cutting line with a pencil or chalk liner. Using scissors, cut through fabric only on pencil line. Repeat for all sides. **Note:** You may have to snip a few stitches where sewing lines intersect.
9. With right sides together and raw edges even, sew through backing and needlepunch, joining logs to form Row 2. Press.
10. Again following diagram on page 22, mark and cut Row 2. Draw line; lift fabric slightly and carefully cut with scissors.
11. Continue in this manner until all rows are completed. **Note:** Row 7 has 2 logs and these are sewn to the sides only.
12. Trim all edges even.
13. Bind with straight strips of fabric. Make gentle pleats to accommodate angles (see Glossary of Techniques on page 73).

Carl Murray

Place Mats *by Nancy Smith and Lynda Milligan, 1989, Denver, Colorado, 14" x 18". A "quilt-as-you-go" technique makes these place mats, which would make an elegant table setting, easy and quick.*

Glossary of Techniques

MACHINE PIECING

1. Make actual-size templates from patterns, if given. If using the template-free method, cut strips with rotary cutter and ruler. Patterns include ¼″ seam allowances unless otherwise noted.
2. Mark the required number of pieces on the wrong side of the fabric, drawing exactly around template. Pieces can be layer cut, if cut accurately.
3. Use a light neutral thread when sewing most fabrics, but if all fabric is dark, use dark thread.
4. Using ¼″ seam allowances, place the pieces that are to be joined with right sides together. Pin, matching seam lines, and sew with a straight stitch (10–12 stitches per inch). Press seam allowances to one side unless otherwise noted.
5. Chain stitch when possible to save time and thread. To chain stitch, sew one seam but do not lift presser foot or cut threads. Take next piece and insert under presser foot as close to last piece as possible. Continue sewing this seam by letting feed dog grip the fabric and pull the pieces through. Sew as many pieces as you can in this manner. Clip pieces apart.
6. Where two seams come together, allow one to fall in one direction and the other in the opposite direction (opposing seams). Butt the seams together exactly. They will hold each other in place, match perfectly, and distribute the fabric evenly.

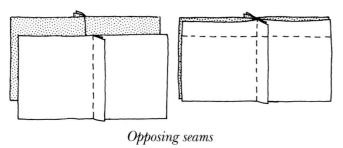

Opposing seams

7. When crossing triangular intersecting seams, aim for the point where the lines intersect. This will keep your points from being cut off.

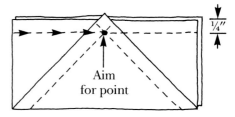

Aim for point

Triangular intersect

8. Finger press or press lightly as you sew, pressing seams toward darker fabric, where possible. Avoid excessive pressing as it tends to stretch fabric out of shape. Do not press seams open. When several seams come together (such as on star points), try to distribute fabric by pressing in a clockwise or counterclockwise direction.

PRESSING

In quilting, all seam allowances are pressed to one side or the other. The standard ¼″ seam allowance used in quiltmaking makes it difficult, if not impossible, to press seams open. In addition, the quilt is actually more durable if seam allowances are not pressed open. It is preferable to press seams toward the darker fabric. If this is not possible, make sure dark fabric seams do not show through on the lighter side by trimming a scant amount off the dark seam allowance. Use steam when pressing and move your iron gently in straight motions, rather than "mashing" movements. Swinging your iron back and forth tends to distort and stretch your patchwork. Iron as smoothly as possible. When pressing block seams (i.e., sewing one block to another), press all seams in the same direction for one whole row. On the next row, press all block seams in the other direction. This will allow seams to fall in opposite directions when sewing one row to another row. When ironing row seams, press the entire seam length of the row in the same direction, always being careful not to stretch.

When ironing border seams, press all seams toward outside edges. A final pressing of your quilt top will make it easier to mark your quilting design and let you see any potential problem areas.

ASSEMBLING OR SETTING BLOCKS TOGETHER

Begin by laying out all your quilt blocks. Take a few minutes to stand back and view your arrangement. If using sparsely patterned fabric, you may find an area of concentrated color that you were not expecting. By laying out all blocks, you will have a chance to decide if this is really what you want.

Scrap quilt blocks often need some rearranging. A little bit of red or yellow in one of your fabrics may "pop" out at you, and distributing this "color" around your quilt may make for a much more pleasing arrangement. Be sure to include any sashing or border strips when laying out your blocks.

When you are satisfied with your arrangement, begin sewing all blocks and sashing strips together into rows. Press all seams of the first row in one direction (i.e., to the right). Continue for Row 2 and press these seams in the opposite direction (i.e., to the left). Continue sewing rows and reversing row seams as you press.

Finally sew Row 1 to Row 2, Row 3 to Row 4, Row 5 to Row 6, etc. Then sew units 1–2 to units 3–4, etc. By sewing row units together, you work with less bulk than when sewing individual blocks together. The final row seam will connect the top half of your quilt to the bottom half.

MITERING CORNERS

1. Mitered corners, while not difficult to make, require some patience to achieve a terrific look. Measure the quilt size without borders. Add to this measurement the width of your planned borders plus approximately 2″–4″ for good measure. If using a striped fabric, make sure all strips are cut with the same design. If your quilt consists of more than one border, sew individual borders together first to make

a complete border unit. You may need more fabric, but the corners are much easier to miter.

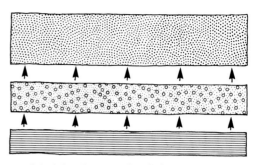

Stitch borders together before mitering

2. Fold quilt and borders in half and mark. Match halfway points and stitch borders to quilt, right sides together. Begin and end stitching ¼″ from corners. Press seam allowances toward outside edges of quilt.

3. Lay quilt on ironing board with right side of quilt up. Work with one corner at a time. You may need to pin quilt to ironing board to keep it from falling off or pulling the corner. With one border overlapping the other, fold it back to a 45° angle. Match the seams or stripes and work with it until it looks good. The outer edges should be very square and without any extra fullness. Seams and pattern lines should create a 90° angle. Press this fold.

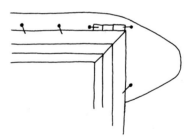

4. Flip top edge of border down onto right edge of border (right sides together), matching edges; pin. Stitch from inner corner (about ⅛″ from seam line). It may be helpful to baste this seam first. Check the seam for accuracy before stitching.

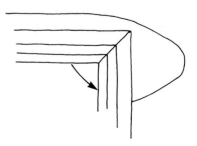

5. Open seam out. If stripes and seams match, press seams open and trim seams to ¼".

MARKING A QUILT TOP

Mark quilt tops before layering them with backing and batting. It is much easier to work on a hard, flat surface. You will need sharp pencils or fine-line chalk markers, quilting stencils or templates, and a straight-edge ruler or ¼" masking tape.

To mark quilt blocks, borders, or sashing strips, use quilt stencils, templates, or ruler and mark lightly with chalk marker or sharp pencils. If using masking tape to mark, care must be taken to remove tape as soon as possible. Follow directions given with particular quilt patterns.

BACKING

Prewash all backing fabric. Use 100% cotton, dress-weight fabric. All-cotton fabric is much easier to quilt through and seldom allows batting fiber to "migrate" through the fabric. Tear off selvages before seaming fabric together. Sheets generally have too high a thread count, making it extremely difficult to hand quilt through.

Seam together pieces of fabric to make a piece large enough to accommodate entire quilt top. The seams can run either horizontally or vertically. The backing should be at least 2" to 3" larger all the way around the quilt top. Press backing seams open. Quilting through one seam layer is much easier than quilting through double-layer seams.

BATTING

Batting is the filler for the quilt and can be 100% cotton, 100% polyester, or a combination of the two. The higher the cotton content, the more closely the quilt must be quilted. Cotton batting usually has no outside covering on it and, thus, will tend to shift. Batting comes in standard bed sizes, from crib size to king size, and may also be purchased by the yard.

BORDER

A separate frame around a pieced or appliqued quilt top, the border is the final statement of a quilt. Borders can repeat fabrics or patterns used in the quilt. They can be pieced or appliqued to enhance the rest of the design, and they can be of any width. Just as a frame can add to or detract from a painting, the border can often "make or break" the total effect of the quilt.

SASHING

These strips of fabric separate individual pieced or appliqued blocks. If the sashing is made in the same fabric as the background, the blocks will appear to float.

BASTING

This step joins the three layers (quilt top, batting, backing) together in preparation for quilting. Basting can be done with safety pins, pinning every few inches but staying away from seams that will be quilted. This method works best for machine quilting. For hand quilting, use a long running stitch, starting in the quilt center and stitching out to the edges in a sunburst design. As you quilt, snip out basting stitches.

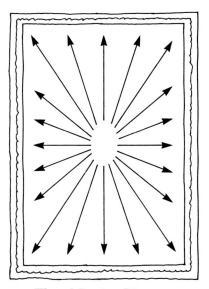

Thread Basting Diagram

QUILTING

Leaving backing and batting slightly larger than quilt, layer backing (wrong side up), batting, and then quilt top (right side up). Baste together from center to the edges in a sunburst design.

Hand quilting is a tiny running stitch, which creates the decorative pattern and holds all three layers in one place. Use a single strand of quilting thread with a tiny knot at one end. Insert needle from the top through quilt top and batting, but not backing. Gently, but firmly, pull the thread from underneath so knot slips through the top layer and lodges in the batting. Bring needle up one stitch length away from beginning spot. Begin with a backstitch. Grasp needle with thumb and forefinger; position thimble at end of needle. Take a few stitches, pushing needle through with the thimble on your middle finger. Use thumb for control. To make sure needle is penetrating all layers, hold other hand directly under so that the tip of your finger actually feels the needle point each time a stitch is taken. To end, make a knot in thread close to last stitch. Insert needle a stitch length away, run needle through batting for a needle's length, and gently pull the thread so knot slips through into batting. Follow desired quilting pattern or outline quilt.

To outline quilt, simply quilt ¼″ out from desired seams. By stitching ¼″ from the seam, you avoid quilting through extra thicknesses of fabric. Generally, quilters feel comfortable "eye-balling" the ¼″; however, an easy way to ensure complete accuracy is to run ¼″

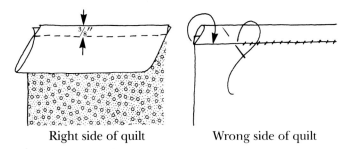

Right side of quilt   Wrong side of quilt

wonderful! Press binding up and over the raw edge so that fold meets stitched line on backing. Pin and stitch by hand.

4. Pin remaining sides as above, except allow the binding to extend ½″ at both ends. Turn the extended portion of the binding down over the bound edge, as illustrated. Finish binding as before.

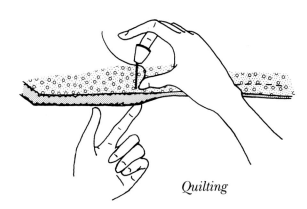

Quilting

masking tape along one side of a seam and then quilt next to the other edge of the tape. When you are finished quilting, you simply pick up the strip of tape and reposition it for another quilting line. This method works equally well for long or short straight lines on borders.

Where directions call for quilting "in the ditch," you simply quilt very close to the seam line on the right side of the quilt. The stitching will show on the back of the quilt, but not on the top. This type of quilting, which can be done by hand or machine, holds the three layers together but does not add another design dimension to the top.

BINDING

We recommend using a double binding because of its durability. You don't need to use bias strips unless you will be going around a curve.

1. Piece ends of 2½″ wide strips to fit along each side. Press the length of binding in half.
2. Working from the right side of the quilt, put binding strips on in the same order as you sewed your borders, or put the two side pieces on first and then the top and bottom pieces.
3. To apply, pin binding to the first two sides of the quilt with raw edges even. Stitch, using a ⅜″ seam and if possible, an even-feed foot on your machine to prevent binding from "scooting" ahead. This attachment helps to feed both top and bottom layers of fabric through your machine at the same time. It's

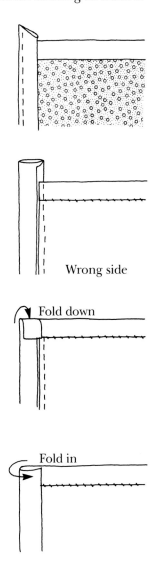

Wrong side

Fold down

Fold in

Cutting and Paste-up Guides

Paste-up Guide

Make 2 copies and tape together on dotted lines.

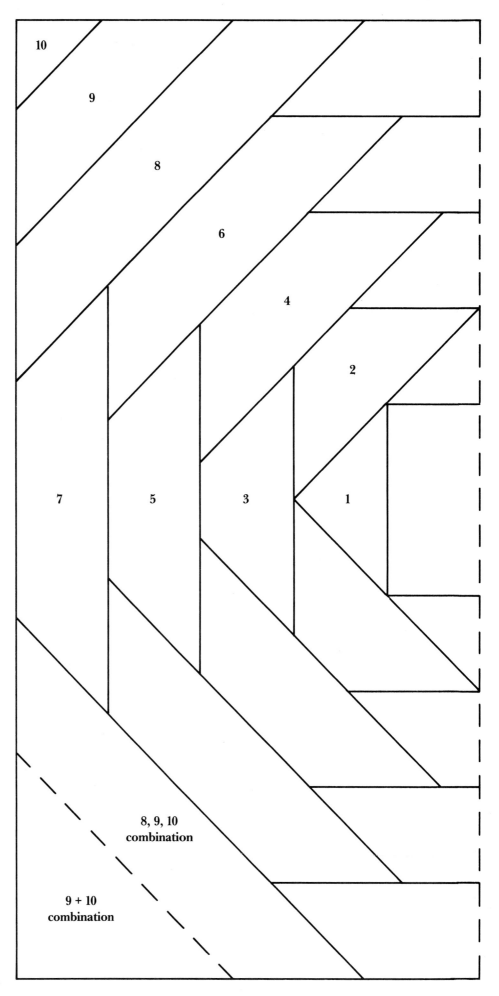

**2″ strip
cutting guide**
(length will vary)

**1½″ strip
cutting guide**
(length will vary)

**3½″ square
cutting guide**

**2½″ square
cutting guide**

Four-Block Coloring Diagrams